HOW TO EARN A LIVING FROM FREELANCE WRITING

An introduction to journalism with set-by-step guides and exercises that teach the craft

SALLY NASH & DEAN STILES

ACKOWLEDGEMENTS

This book is dedicated to the journalists, editors, and sub-editors – too many to name – with whom we have worked and whose inspiration, guidance and advice helped us hone our skills.

CONTENTS

FOREWORD

Thank you for choosing *How to earn a living from freelance writing*. We hope you are keen to get started. This book takes the form of a short, but intensive, course that provides the essential skills to get you started in print and web journalism. It is not an academic book; we are not concerned with the theory of journalism. This is about practical, no nonsense advice and guidance from two experienced journalists who have survived, and enjoyed over twenty years in the trade.

The book is packed with exercises to you hone the techniques and skills you need to start your career in freelance journalism or employed by a publisher. We are confident that if you follow the chapters and do the exercises carefully you will fully understand the basics of news and feature writing and be able to make your first pitch for a commission. It will take about four hours a chapter to do the tasks thoroughly but it is well worth the effort.

Some of you reading this might be looking to switch career. Others might just be looking for a taste of journalism to see if you enjoy it before taking it further. Some people might be looking to add another string to their bow and to earn some extra money alongside their main job. Whatever the reason you will find in this book an excellent practical introduction to the basics of good professional writing.

Sally Nash and Dean Stiles
London 2011

GETTING STARTED

Why journalism?

Why you want to write, as much as your background and experience, will determine what you write about. For some it might be a curiosity and love of current affairs, for others it might be the desire to write about a particular specialist interest. The job is varied and flexible, particularly as a freelance.

The routes into the industry are as many and as varied as its journalists. The distinguished journalist and broadcaster, Andrew Marr, stumbled into journalism because he wanted to do something with his first class English degree. The internationally renowned foreign correspondent Robert Fisk saw Alfred Hitchcock's' film Foreign Correspondent, when aged 12, and knew that was what he wanted to be. David English, deputy director at Cardiff University's Centre for Journalism, has a list of his successful attributes for budding journalists. It includes commitment, enthusiasm, being a news junkie, interested in current affairs and never giving up. "Those who will not take 'no' for an answer will get there in the end."

Journalism and related media jobs are popular with graduates: in 2008 the media topped a list of applications for jobs. Even in 2009, when the recession was influencing career choice, media applications came second at 13.6% of all graduate applications, behind the more secure career choice of teaching.

How this book works

Each chapter comes with advice and guidance on specific skills that you need as a journalist, whether working as a freelance or employed on a newspaper, magazine, or web site. Throughout the chapters, there are examples to illustrate the techniques as well as exercises to practice and improve your skills. It will take about 20 minutes to read the chapter, but about three hours to systematically work through the material, carry out the exercises, and check your work.

Unfortunately, as with any skill worth having, there is no easy route to success. And there are no short cuts. But by following the chapters and completing the exercises you will see your writing improve and this will strengthen your motivation and resolve.

Each chapter ends with a revision exercise designed to test the knowledge and skill that you have acquired. This is the most important of the exercises and the one to spend that little bit more time working on. As a journalist, you need to write accurately but also quickly. The exercises will help you increase your writing speed. We set time limits on many of the exercises to help you increase your writing speed.

What the book provides

The book is designed to provide a grounding in journalism, teaching the basic skills necessary to get started as a freelance or to be able to apply with confidence for a job on a magazine, website or newspaper.

This book, although designed for would-be journalists, also provides an excellent grounding for any form of writing whether a business report or even a novel. Author, Tim Clare, had the following to say to aspiring novelists: "Cutting back on adjectives and adverbs while leaving beefed-up nouns and verbs to carry the load sometimes produces a clipped, journalistic kind of prose, but it's far better than a tangled mass of flowery description."

It is that "clipped journalistic prose" that we will teach you. In Chapter three we explore the language of journalism, where we teach you to dump the adjectives, get the verbs working, and make every word count.

Journalism is a craft, not a profession. Journalism requires basic skills that take many hours to perfect and polish. More simply, the more you write the better your writing. This is why each chapter includes numerous exercises. These are for your benefit but do not cheat and skip them! They are the means for you to practice the techniques described.

This course is only the start of your learning. As you work for more titles and publications, your experience will increase. There is always more to learn, especially in an industry being shaped by new technology like the Internet and now the increasing array of other means of accessing the Internet apart from desk top computers, like mobile phones, smart phones and yet more still to be dreamed up.

Who needs qualifications?

To become a journalist twenty years ago, training was compulsory and provided by newspapers, mostly local newspapers. Everyone had to pass examinations set by the National Council for the Training of Journalists (NCTJ). Like the printing trade, it was a closed shop. Journalists had to spend at least two years on provincial papers before venturing, if they had the talent, to Fleet Street where national newspapers were then based.

That has all changed: today journalism in Britain, unlike the United States, is free of entry restrictions. It is cheerfully chaotic, unstructured and wonderfully unprofessional; a free-for-all where the best writers succeed. There is no accepted career structure, no salary scale, and it is full of charlatans and other dubious characters. But that is what makes it so exciting. Journalists, even humble ones on small specialist titles, access the most powerful in the land: top business leaders and decision makers in almost every facet of life.

There is a huge array of courses out there from short e-courses at a few hundred pounds to three-year degrees with fees in excess of £15,000. What do you get for your money? Certainly no guarantee of a job. Nor is a degree is essential. In fact many argue that degree courses are too long and too expensive for what is now not that well paid a career. You will see jobs advertised specifying NCTJ (National Council for Training) training as a minimum. But editors do not look for qualifications from freelance journalists. The reason is simple: editors do not need to rely on certificates to access your skill: they merely look at your writing. They want good copy. This book will help you write to the standards expected.

Learning on the job, the traditional route for many journalists is much harder than was previously the case with few publishers offering training. The book allows you to taste a career as a journalist and to see whether you have some natural ability. If nothing else, you will emerge after a few weeks able to write far better than before – a powerful and useful skill that is always useful.

Journalism as a career

Estimates put the number of journalists in the UK at 100,000, working in print, radio, television, public relations, advertising, and probably many more outlets. It says a lot about the craft that there are no exact figures.

At the top of the tree are the editors of national newspapers earning £500,000 or more. Next in line, and often earning more than the editors of their newspapers, are the star columnists like Simon Jenkins, who writes for the *Guardian*, and Richard Littlejohn on the *Sun*.

Less well known are the ranks of section editors, supplement editors, and specialist reporters. They are well paid but work hard with long hours and are involved as much with management issues, such as budgets and commissioning, as with writing. Below them are the specialist political editors, reporters, critics, and others who work doggedly, improving their craft and their contacts. They earn good salaries and are the backbone of their newspapers.

From here, there is a huge drop into the world of local newspapers and magazines and web sites and where you will be working, certainly initially. The great bulk of journalists are employed on small magazines, web sites and free sheets, in advertising and public relations where pay is poor: salaries are often less than £15,000 and rarely over £40,000 even for magazine editors. Freelance earnings are difficult to assess but usually fall within this range.

Many people come into journalism in their late teens or early twenties only to then leave after a decade or two for jobs in public relations, teaching, and other careers. Apart from the select few, journalism is not well paid. Its rewards are in doing something you love, working among people you know well. But for the freelance, it can be a lonely life since few editors will pay expenses for travel. For much of the time life is lived on the telephone and in front of a screen tapping away at the keyboard.

The journalist and broadcaster, Andrew Marr, sums up journalism as "a carnival of insecurity where teetotallers are less successful than they expect." He wrote: "I have worked alongside the children of immigrants from the Caribbean and Uganda; working class Marxists; former Army officers; novelists; at least one former Irish terrorist; hopeless alcoholics and serial drug abusers; vegetarian anarchists; dissipated aristocrats; anger-fuelled men who left school at sixteen; refugees from the law, the City, and from factory lines; fastidious professionals who cared about the truthfulness of every phrase they used; and sloppy, cynical liars." Welcome to the world of journalism. There is certainly a place for you!

Let's get started

Enough background, let's get down to work and explore your interests and get you writing. This first chapter is a fun introduction to the world of journalism and the craft of writing stories. As with all chapters, the value is not solely in reading and digesting the information given but the means to get you writing for a specific purpose. A novelist may spend a year planning and plotting before they put pen to paper: not so with journalism where you write to demand regardless of how creative you feel on a particular day. Just as truck drivers do not suffer 'driver's block', there is no such thing as 'writer's block' for a journalist.

Getting started is often the most difficult task for a trainee journalist. So, we have set exercises that appear throughout each chapter and designed to reinforce your learning and to help you start writing immediately. Part of the craft of being a journalist is to become an instant expert on anything. Your skill is researching a topic and finding information that you present in words to an audience through a magazine, newspaper, or web site. But all journalists develop a speciality and bring to bear a vast range of knowledge to the topic. It takes time to acquire this and for the trainee journalist it is a case of having to start somewhere.

In this chapter, you will identify a subject, find an outlet for your work, identify an idea for an article, and write at least the opening part of that story. To help you we have devised a series of exercises to work through each stage. Let's start.

Exercise 1

The advice given to aspiring novelists is to write about what they know, initially at least: the same is true for trainee journalists. So, in what subject area do you have an interest or any special knowledge? Is it poetry, sewing, railways, computers, sailing, football, photography, singing, painting, music, politics, the environment, low carbon housing...? Choose a subject that you enjoy or where you have expertise or specialist knowledge and write the answer on your notepad. That is exercise one done. Who said training to be a journalist was hard?

The market for journalism

If you look at the range of magazines and newspapers on sale at a newsagent you will know that the print market is vast, like the Internet. There are millions of words on every conceivable subject. Magazines and newspapers employ staff writers and buy immense amounts of material to fill their pages and web sites. Somewhere out there is scope for you to sell your writing. Considering the size and scale of print media, you may be surprised that there is no formal system for buying and selling copy.

There are literary agents who sell work on behalf of writers charging a commission, as much as 30% of the fee paid by the publisher. Some writing schools work in this manner, which is how they can claim to get your work published. Most editors prefer to use their own informal network of writers, people whose work they know and whose skill they trust. Breaking into that network is the challenge for the aspiring writer. Now that you have established what you want to write about, we need to define a target market and to select from the myriad titles and websites out there, which ones suit you.

Exercise 2

Bearing in mind your chosen subject area, visit a newsagent, preferably a large one like W H Smith, and check the newspapers and magazines on sale to identify which would be likely to include a story about your special subject. If you cannot get to a newsagent check for titles on subscription websites, like www.magazinesubscription.co.uk/ or www.subscription.co.uk/, or www.isubscribe.co.uk/.

Now write a list of at least six magazine or newspaper titles. This is your target print market. If you find that you have too many possible titles then your subject area is too wide. You need to be very precise, so if you have decided that writing about politics is your thing, you need to specify what aspect of politics, such as social reform, children's issues, policing, and so on.

What about the web?

In a very short time the Internet has grow exponentially. It is a new technology, continually evolving and as such offers new writers huge opportunity to get started, to promote themselves, and to find an audience for their work. You may well want to concentrate solely on the Internet. However, bear in mind that most publishers are still locked into print versions of their publications and tend to transfer print material to the Internet as much as they create directly for web sites. The entry point for you, in many cases, is still the publishers' print edition.

Exercise 3

You have identified print media outlets. Now search the Internet for websites about your specialist subject area. Write a list of at least six web sites but exclude those that are web sites for print products already identified in the previous exercise. You are looking for stand-alone web sites that contain lots of articles, news stories, and reports. All this material has to come from somewhere and there may be scope for you to provide some of it.

What's my style?

So far, you know your subject area: you have identified a target market of print tiles and web sites. That selection will start to determine the type of material that you will write and the language style you need to use. Finding your voice, as prose writers call it, takes time and practice. But unlike novel writing, in journalism the medium dictates your voice.

Exercise 4

Revisit those titles and web sites that you identified and note what type of material they would most likely use about your subject. You need to be assessing each to see whether they take news stories, feature articles, illustrated features, gossip, product reviews, 'how to' articles etc.

In later chapters we will talk in more detail about how you assess outlets for your work because you also need to establish how and where your chosen outlets sources its copy: do they have staff writers, do they use freelances, is it supplied free by enthusiasts? At this stage we will assume they will take freelance material, and more importantly, that they pay for such material.

Exercise 5

You know your subject, the outlet for your work, and the style of story. You must now decide what that story is about. You need to write a synopsis, a short, 80 or so word outline of the story and give it a title. In Chapter Eight, you will see that this is the basis of all pitches to editors when you sell your work.

Here is an example: It is 83 words long and for an article in a specialist, monthly, railway preservation magazine read mainly by people working within the industry but also by enthusiasts and volunteer workers.

Title: Open Door Steam Fest
Synopsis: Why the Blue Bell Railway has put money back into preservation steam railways. The Blue Bell's innovative "workshop open doors days", that allow visitors to get hands-on experience in the repair workshops, have led to a 20% increase in visitor numbers, and mostly revenue-generating adult visitors too. The article to interview the general manager at the Blue Bell

Railway about how the open door sessions work, and include comments from visitors attending a recent workshop open day.

Now write the synopsis for your idea for an article. You need to come up with a title that will provoke the editor's interest then state what the story is about (the angle), why it is worth writing (what is different), and who you plan to interview. In Chapter Eight we will return to the synopsis you have written and we guarantee that you will be able to write it again, but shorter, snappier, and in a real attention-grabbing style.

How to write

And now we come to crux of the matter: how to write the article. This is the hard part and the basis for much of book course. In the next eight chapters we will systematically show you the techniques and skills necessary to write effectively and to the standard demanded by most publications and web sites.

We do not claim that by the end of the book you will be writing to the standard of leader writers of the *Times, Guardian, Mail* or *Mirror* where you can see some of the highest standards of writing and journalism. But, at the very least, at the end of this book you will be able to write in a good, workmanlike style more than adequate for most publications and web sites. Writing, like journalism, is a craft, and with practice your skill will improve and your writing will evolve, taking on a unique style of your own.

Revision exercise

It is now time for the final exercise in this chapter. Write the first 350 words of the article that you identified in exercise five. Here are some tips to get you going.

> • *do not try to write the perfect introduction first. Just start writing and the introduction will come later*
> • *cannot start? Then ask yourself, "What is the story?" Write the answer, it is usually your first sentence*
> • *do not get carried away with fancy language. Just say what you need to say simply and clearly*
> • *think each sentence through in your head before you type. If it is too long to remember, it is too long to use*
> • *set out an outline of the story with brief subject headings before you start writing. This helps your story flow with each sentence leading to the next.*

Further reading

William Deedes, *At War with Waugh: The Real Story of "Scoop"*, Pan Books (2004)

William Deedes, *Words and Deedes: Selected Journalism 1931-2006*, Pan Books (2007)

Simon Jenkins, *The Market for Glory: Fleet Street Ownership in the Twentieth Century*, Faber and Faber (1986)

Phillip Knightley, *The First Casualty*, The John Hopkins University Press, (Baltimore 2004)

Phillip Knightley, *A Hack's Progress*, Vintage (1998)

Andrew Marr, *My Trade - A Short History of British Journalism*, Pan Macmillan (London 2005)

Evelyn Waugh, *Scoop: A Novel About Journalists*, Penguin Classics (2003)

Jim Willis, *The Mind of a Journalist: How Reporters View Themselves, Their World, and Their Craft*, Sage Publications (2009)

Web sites

http://www.britishpapers.co.uk/category/trade/

A listing of newspapers, magazines, and other titles in Britain

http://www.bjr.org.uk/index

The British Journalism Review: a forum of analysis and debate with topical articles covering all areas of the profession

HOW TO WRITE NEWS

News writing is a key skill for journalists – probably the key skill. Understanding how to write a news story is the foundation for writing everything else, from press releases to reports. News writing is about telling a story concisely and accurately. And as news writing follows a basic formula, anyone can learn how to do this with a bit of help and guidance. While styles can diverge more dramatically depending on the kind of story – a feature story may look and sound very different from a hard news one – all news stories are cut from the same mould.

What is a news story?
The clue is in the question. Let us take the dictionary definition of news:
- recent events; important or interesting recent happenings
- information about such events, as in the mass media.

From our point of view, it is the "important or interesting recent happenings" that we need to focus on.

You need to acquire a "nose for news" which is the ability to spot how information can be turned into a story. Start by thinking about recent happenings and consider which you would include in a news bulletin on the BBC or other news service.

Exercise 1

Can you list three "important or interesting recent happenings" to have hit the UK news headlines over the last week. Put them in order of importance. For example, in the week of writing this chapter, I could have selected:

1) Resignation of the House of Commons speaker, Michael Martin
2) Government announces an interim package of measures on MP's expenses
3) Calls for a general election

This was an exciting week for news: it is not always this good! Identify the three most newsworthy stories of the current week. Write your answers on a notepad.

What's in a news story

Neil Hopp is the former writing coach at the Northwest Herald in Crystal Lake, US. Here is Hopp's first five formula for news.

A news story should always have:
- an effective lead - focused, short, and memorable
- a second paragraph that amplifies the lead
- a third paragraph that continues to build detail
- following paragraphs that provide context or tell reader why this is important
- a power quote. An interesting quote that propels meaning: not just a fluffy quote that gets in the way.

Hierarchies and news story structure

Monarchies, the military, and schools all conform to a hierarchy; that is, they are all ordered in terms of importance.

Journalism instructors usually describe the organisation or structure of a news story as an inverted pyramid. This means that the journalist top-loads the essential and most interesting elements of his or her story, with supporting information following in order of diminishing importance.

This structure enables readers to stop reading at any point and still come away with the essence of a story. The inverted pyramid structure also enables articles to be cut to any arbitrary length during page layout, to fit in the space available.

Inexperienced writers are often told: "Don't bury the lead!" This is to ensure that they present the most important facts first, rather than requiring the reader to go through several paragraphs to find them. In such an approach, the first line, or lead, must convey what the news is.

But according to US newspaper the *Northern Star*, news stories do not have to follow the old, worn-out, inverted pyramid format. You will still use it sometimes, particularly for important, breaking news on deadline. But look for opportunities to veer from that format into something more interesting. Never forget, though, says the *Northern Star*, that your number one objective is to tell people what they need to know - not to show them how much of a literary artist you are.

Exercise Two
Read the following news article.

Landmark UK case tests pre-nuptial principle By Megan Murphy and Sujata Das, 20 April 2009

One of Germany's wealthiest women is seeking to enforce a pre-nuptial agreement that would leave her former investment banker husband with nothing in the latest landmark divorce case to hit British courts.

Katrin Radmacher, a paper industry heiress worth an estimated £100m, claims that her estranged spouse is trying to renege on a deal made before they married in London in 1998, in which he agreed not to make a claim against her in the event of a separation.

If she is successful, the case could overturn the long-standing principle that pre-nuptial contracts, widely recognised in Europe and the US, are not legally binding in England.

Her estranged husband, Nicolas Granatino, has hired Fiona Shackleton, one of London's most feared divorce lawyers, to represent him at the Court of Appeal next week.

The case marks a bitter end for a romance that started at Tramp, the members-only nightclub in Mayfair. Mr Granatino, a French national who formerly earned as much as $470,000 a year with J P Morgan, gave up his banking career about six years ago to pursue a doctorate in biotechnology at Oxford.

The couple's marriage broke down shortly afterwards, culminating in a formal separation in 2006. He says he now expects to earn just £30,000 a year as an academic researcher and has accumulated debts totalling several hundred thousand pounds.

Under the terms of their pre-nuptial agreement, executed under German law four months before their marriage, both parties agreed not to make any financial claim against each other if they split up.

As part of the divorce proceedings in July, a UK High Court judge ruled it would be "manifestly unfair" to hold Mr Granatino to the deal given their respective financial strength and ordered Ms Radmacher to make a one-off lump sum payment of £5.6m.

Ms Radmacher is challenging that decision in a case likely to have far-reaching consequences for other globetrotting couples who choose to make their home in London, the so-called divorce capital of the world.

Julian Lipson, a divorce lawyer at Withers in London, said: "The English courts pride themselves on protecting the financially weaker party and that will override the argument that the financially weaker spouse knew what they were signing and should be held to the bargain, even if it is a bad one."

Let us analyse this news story, particularly the opening two paragraphs:
1 Does it answer the five Ws and the H (see box, page 3)?
Who is?   What?   Where?   When?   Why?   How?
2 Now write the answers to these questions as shown in the article and indicate where they appear in the story.

The crux of all news

The Five "W"s and the "H". This is the crux of all news - these six words.

Who? What? Where? When? Why? How?

It does not matter how you remember these six key words but it is important to remember them. You should be able to answer most, if not all, of these in the introduction to a news story.

The poet and writer Rudyard Kipling he of Jungle Book fame had something to say about this:

> I keep six honest serving men
> (They taught them all I knew);
> Their names are names are What and Why and When
> And How and Where and Who.

Beyond the introduction

After the introduction, the rest of the news article explains and expands on the beginning, giving the reader more and more information in order of decreasing importance. The last section of the story contains the least essential information – the details of the piece. If your news story needs to be shorter because you have written too much or there is suddenly less space, the sub-editor will cut from the bottom. If your most important point or angle is at the end, then you no longer have a 'news' story and it will not make sense.

Quotations

Most of the quotations that you use will come from face-to-face, telephone, or e-mail interviews, press releases, and company statements. Remember to use quotes only if they contain unique information that only your source could say. For example, in a story about a shipping accident you would not quote the shipping engineer saying: "The ship was built in 1972". This is a fact, not a unique statement. That fact that the ship was built in 1972 is on record and can be verified easily. This information, if it were relevant, would be included as a statement in the story, not as a quote.

Do not scatter quotes randomly in the story. Quotes are devices that tell the story using the words of the source. Plan your story and use an outline to determine where to place appropriate quotes. In the case of our shipping story, if paragraph two is to discuss concerns about flooding when the ship was built, this is the place to include the quote from an engineer saying, "No one listened when I said there could be a problem if the bow doors weren't closed. They said I was an alarmist. And now look what's happened."

Balance your use of quotes. If you are reporting a controversial story, try to include a more or less equal number of quotes from each side. This will not necessarily stop someone from complaining, but at least you will be able to point out that you tried to tell each side of the story. In the shipping story, the engineer's quote should be balanced with something from the ship owner or builder, perhaps stating that the ship met all relevant standards.

Use direct quotes to make a boring article come to life. You could paraphrase what your source said and write, "Princess Diana said that she was afraid that her car would be involved in an accident and she would die," but it is much more effective to quote Diana saying, ""My husband is planning 'an accident' in my car." When including a direct quote, make sure you correctly cite the person who said it.

Clarity in news
Five tips about writing
- Journalism is not academic writing. We do not use big words, long sentences and paragraphs to show our readers how smart we are
- Readers are pressed for time. You have to give them the news quickly, concisely and without unnecessary words or information
- Every story competes for a reader's attention ... against other stories, the TV in the background, the Internet and against every distraction you can think of
- With every story you write, ask yourself: What is the news here? Why should my readers care? What does this mean to them? Your lead, and then the rest of your story, should spring from those questions. Then, ask yourself "What questions will the reader have that I need to answer?"
- Write short sentences, short paragraphs, and short stories. Use simple language. Think hard about every word you use.

The do's and don'ts of news writing

Do not forget people

News stories are all about how people are affected by events. In your financial story about interest rates, you might spend some time focusing on who this will affect: if interest rates go down then pensioners' income from savings might be reduced but mortgage repayments will be less.

Have an angle

Most stories can be presented using a particular angle or "slant". Many regional newspapers will take a national story and obtain a regional angle. For example, the chancellor's budget statement is a national story but local business people, pensioners, and taxpayers will all have a view on it, peculiar to the area.

Keep it objective

The writer must be impartial. Cover all sides to a story. This is particularly important when covering any contentious story. If you are giving a trade union view about a company's redundancies, for example, make sure you give the firm a "right of reply". If the company will not comment or could not be reached, say so at the end of the piece. Company X declined to comment. Or nobody from company X was available to comment. It shows that you have at least tried to get a response from them and this, as well as being fair, could be critical if you have a legal problem later.

Don't use I and me

Unless you are quoting someone. And speaking of quoting...

Quote People

For example: "We have no choice but to cut 10% of our workforce," said chief executive Paul Turner of Acme Finance. "We hope to achieve this through voluntary redundancies."

No Purple Prose

Keep your sentences and paragraphs short. If you find your sentences stretching out to include clauses and sub clauses, then it is probably time to begin a new sentence. Do not use lots of heavily descriptive language. When you have finished, go through the story and try to remove any words that are not completely necessary, usually adjectives.

Keep it active

Seize those verbs. Make them work for you, not trailing behind a stream of multi-syllabic nouns or adjectives. Use short, snappy, precise words. Avoid foreign words, jargon, technical words, abbreviation, and puns that can mystify readers. The last thing you want is to stop your readers in their tracks. Avoid slang: it diminishes the value of your story and makes it less credible.

Exercise Three

Let us try writing the introduction to a news story. Take the facts listed below and select the most newsworthy. Do not forget that your introduction should be short and pithy, and contain as many of the what, why, who, where, when, etc, as possible.

1) Read the list of facts below. These are not in any order.
2) Choose and place in order of importance for a news story.
3) Write the first sentence of the news story. Remember, 30-words maximum.

• The BMW and the motorcycle have been recovered by the police but officers are still searching for the other cars. The registration plates for the Mercedes - LV06 HFA - and the Volkswagen - RA07 XEV - are known to be cloned but police have appealed to anyone who spots them to report it.
• Officers also found a loaded handgun in connection with the incident although it was not the gun fired outside the store.
• Police investigating Britain's biggest jewel heist yesterday announced a £1m reward for any information leading to the arrests of the suspects. They took a female staff member hostage and fired two warning shots at members of the public as they made their getaway.
• Two armed men stole £40m worth of diamond rings, necklaces and watches during a daytime raid on the Graff jewellery store in Mayfair on 6 August.

• Once inside the New Bond Street store the men, wearing latex disguises, stole 43 items before making off in a blue BMW. One of the men was seen to hand a package to a man on a motorcycle. They then abandoned the BMW and changed to a Mercedes and switched again into a Volkswagen Sharan.

• The men caused mayhem as they left the scene, firing a gun as they made their way to a BMW.

• The smartly dressed pair, whose raid on Graffs of Mayfair was one of the biggest crimes ever committed in Britain, stole 43 pieces of jewellery worth an estimated £40 million last Thursday.

Exercise Four

Now go through the story from the previous exercise and check it against the following criteria:

1) Style: Is it written in an objective way?

2) Length: Have you written to length? If the opening sentence is over 32 words go back to the drawing board!

3) Does it fulfil the Who, What, Where, When, Why, How formula? Or as much as is possible without sacrificing sense?

If you have missed any of these, re-write or correct your story to suit.

Exercise Five

The editor of School Lunches Today has asked you to write a 350-word news article based on the press release shown below. But she only wants you to use the bare minimum of information contained in the release. She wants you to focus on one particular school. Write a list of possible interviewees and then the questions you would ask for this piece. How would you take the story in a different direction?

Press Release: School meals back on the menu for children in England (09/07/09)

Historic decline in school meals numbers halted.
The first statistically robust national survey of school meal take up has shown that meal numbers have increased in both primary and secondary schools in 2008/9 when compared to identical local authority data for the period 2007/8.

Figures in primary schools increased from 43.8% to 43.9% and from 35.5% to 36.0% in secondary schools for those authorities that reported using the new standardised take up methodology in both 2007/8 and 2008/9.

With all local authorities who responded included, the overall national take up take up figures were 39.3% in primary schools and 35.1% in secondary schools. These figures cannot be directly compared with any previous data due to the range and method of collection (see notes below).

Prue Leith, Chair of the School Food Trust, said: "We now have a genuine picture of take up across the country and we can see that real progress is being made the length and breadth of England. I am absolutely delighted that three million children are eating healthy, nutritionally balanced school food every day.

"I am heartened that take up has increased slightly in primary schools following the introduction of new nutrient-based standards and am convinced we are winning the battle for the hearts, minds and taste buds of children and parents. It is particularly pleasing that secondary schools have turned the corner.

"This has always been a long-term project which relies on the support of cooks, caterers, LAs and head teachers. We must continue to get all schools to regard children's food as an integral part of their overall education so our children will not only be healthier but, as our new research shows, will also be able to perform better".

Neil Porter, Chairman of the Local Authority Caterers Association (LACA), said: "LACA recognises that this year we are using a different way to calculate the data on the take up of school lunches. LACA is encouraged by the apparent marginal upward trend in meal take up in both primary and secondary schools.

"LACA is encouraged by the signs from the Survey that children's eating habits are beginning to turn around, thanks to the hard work of schools and caterers. However, we believe that we are on a longer journey when it comes to secondary school students. Increasing secondary meal take up will continue to be a challenge for all of us. We need to focus on improving partnerships with Head Teachers, encouraging whole school food policies and demonstrating to young people the benefits of choosing healthier food."

Ends

News contacts and sources

For most news writers on a magazine or newspaper, developing contacts is a must. Job adverts for journalists - especially on women's magazines - tend to ask for people with a "bulging contacts book". Whether they are regional union contacts or helpful PRs, getting contacts to trust you is a good way of getting some news. So starting to build a telephone, website and e-mail contact list is a good idea, the earlier the better.

Every journalist is trying to get the "off diary" story: this is where you are not using a press release, statement etc that is released to all and sundry but a story that you have sourced yourself. This is often from a phone call, still the best way of obtaining information that you would not have got anywhere else.

Exercise Six

You are doing a morning shift at a regional newspaper, the Oxford News. You are asked to call the local police to see if anything news-worthy is going on. Sergeant Jon Cass tells you the following:

• a man had been found murdered outside the Black Swan, on Temple Road in Cowley.

• the police are now looking for two white youths aged around 20-25.

• witnesses described how the murdered man had been taunted throughout the night and eventually got involved in a fight.

Other facts:

• *the murdered man is believed to be a soldier, in between stints in Afghanistan and Iraq.*

• *he leaves a wife and three children.*

• *the pub was at the centre of another incident a year ago when a man was stabbed though survived.*

• *as the policeman signs off, he says: "Oh, and one of the witnesses believes that one of the attackers could be the son of a local MP."*

It is 11:30 in the morning. You have 30 minutes to bang out the story for a noon deadline so there is just enough time to make a phone call. For this exercise:

   1) Who would you call?

   2) What will you ask?

   3) Write a 250-word news story using the information you have gained from your imaginary interview as well as the information we have provided.

Exercise Seven

The following sentences are from a report by a Sheffield paper. The sentences are not in any order. Write a 230-word news story, suitable for a Sheffield newspaper, using the information provided but in a suitable news hierarchy.

Life for prison plot murder gang
The men began chanting as they were taken from the court.
Four gang members have been jailed for life after being found guilty of the murder of a Sheffield teenager.
Tarek Chaiboub, 17, was shot outside a barber shop in Burngreave in July 2008.
After five days of deliberations a jury found Michael Chattoo, 21, Nigel Ramsey, 23, Denzil Ramsey, 20, and Levan Menzies, 17, guilty of murder.
Tarek's killing was ordered by gang leader Nigel Ramsey on a smuggled mobile phone from inside prison, the trial at Sheffield Crown Court heard.
The teenager was carrying a handgun at the time of his death.

The full rigour of the law must be brought to bear and rogues like you must be brought to book enunciated Mr Justice Griffith Williams

Nigel Ramsey, of Andover Street, was told he would serve a minimum of 35 years in prison. Chattoo, of Daniel Hill Street, will serve at least 30 years, while Denzil Ramsey, who lived with his brother in Andover Street, will serve at least 25 years behind bars. Menzies, also of Andover Street, will serve a minimum of 20 years.

Sentencing Mr Justice Griffith Williams said: "Britain is not broken, although certain communities are being plagued by the lawless activities of the likes of you and gangs such as S3.

"I make it clear that to protect them the full rigour of the law must be brought to bear and rogues like you brought to book."

Chattoo, Nigel Ramsey and Javan Galloway, 20, were also all found guilty of attempted murder in relation to a knife attack on Tarek days before he was killed.

Galloway, of Nottingham Street, was given a nine-year term in a young offenders' institution and told he must serve at least half of the sentence.

The defendants had all denied the allegations against them.

The teenager died from bullet wounds to his back.

Nigel Ramsey and Chattoo smiled and exchanged remarks as the sentences were handed down by Mr Justice Griffith Williams.

As the group left the dock they started chanting and shouting. Outside the court, two women were arrested amid scuffles with police and bystanders.

The two attacks on Tarek happened as part of a feud between members of the city's S3 gang, named after the postcode of the districts of Burngreave and Pitsmoor in Sheffield.

The feud stemmed from the murder of gang member Brett Blake a month earlier, the trial heard.

Outside court Tarek's father Rashid Chaiboub stood by an interpreter who read a statement which said: "Our son Tarek used to have lots of friends and his main mistake was that he trusted some of those who should not be trusted.

"They handed him the death sentence and, for his family and his friends, the life sentence."

ENDS

Check your facts

• As a reporter, you have a lot of power. Get a fact wrong, misspell a name or omit a vital piece of information and you are in danger of not only misinforming the public, but of damaging the credibility of the newspaper or magazine. Always double-check facts

•You might be forgiven for minor errors in a news story - but getting someone's name wrong is unforgivable!

• Always check titles, dates and place names. The sub-editor will not know if the name is correct

• Always check name spellings. For example there is Ian and Iain, Stephen and Steven, Graham and Graeme, Rachel and Rachael.... and so on

• Check your facts with another person and check figures, data and statistics with published sources. The web is fantastic tool but it is not gospel either.

Exercise Eight

This exercise is about finding the news hidden in a press release. Journalists routinely take stories handed to them by press releases, as a quick scan of any newspaper will rapidly reveal. According to research commissioned by Nick Davies at Cardiff University, about 80% of news coverage is rehashed from press releases.

However, as little as a single telephone call can add useful information to that in the press release, turning the story from a re-hash into a much more interesting and useful news item.

For exercise eight:
1) Write a 250-word news story for the Daily Mail, based on the following press release.
2) If you were to research this story further:
1) What angle would you take?
2) Who would you want to interview?

Press Release:

Decline in Homicides Due To Mental Disorder Linked to Improvements in Psychiatric Treatment, UK

Improvements in psychiatric treatments have been cited as a likely reason for the decline in homicide rates due to mental disorder in the last 30 years.

In a study published in the August issue of the British Journal of Psychiatry, researchers re-examined the official homicide statistics from England and Wales between 1946 and 2004.

Analysis revealed that the rate of total homicide and the rate of homicide due to mental disorder rose steadily until the mid-1970s.

The data showed that the annual number of homicides due to mental disorder rose from under 50 in 1957, to well above 100 by the 1970s. The highest annual rate of 0.235 per 100,000 population was in 1973 and the absolute number peaked in 1979. Between 1957 and 1980, homicides due to mental disorder and total homicides were strongly correlated.

However, in the subsequent 24 years (1981-2004), homicides due to mental disorder declined and were negatively correlated with the rate of homicide by people without mental disorder. In other words, there was a reversal in the rate of homicides attributed to mental disorder, which declined to historically low levels, while other homicides continued to rise.

The absolute number of homicides due to mental disorder fell to levels not seen since the early 1950s, and the rate has been at historic lows of 0.07 per 100,000 population or lower since 2000.

The authors observed that the reasons for the rise and fall in homicides attributed to mental disorder are not clear cut. One possible explanation may have been changes in the threshold for the finding of a verdict of diminished responsibility, the largest group of such homicides. However, there have been no changes to the official definitions of the defences to murder since the reforms of the mid-1950s.

Another possibility is that methods of detecting mental disorder before trial have changed over the past 50 years. But, if anything, the detection of mental illness among prisoners is more likely to have improved over this time and it seems unlikely that there has been a decline in the ability of courts to detect the role of mental disorder.

Instead, the researchers propose that the decline in homicide rate attributed to mental disorder is due to improvements in treatment and in service organisation. The introduction and increasing use of antipsychotic medication, the greater awareness of the treatment of psychosis by primary care providers after deinstitutionalisation, and the creation of regional health authorities with responsibility for defined populations, may have all contributed to the observed decline in homicide since the 1970s.

This reasoning is also consistent with the findings of recent studies in the UK and Australia, which suggest that initial treatment of psychosis may reduce the risk of homicide.

Reference:
Homicide due to mental disorder in England and Wales over 50 years
Large M, Smith G, Swinson N, Shaw J and Neilssen O (2008)
British Journal of Psychiatry, 193: 130-133

The Royal College of Psychiatrists is the professional and educational body for psychiatrists in the United Kingdom and the Republic of Ireland. We promote mental health by:
    - Setting standards and promoting excellence in mental health care
        - Improving understanding through research and education
        - Leading, representing, training and supporting psychiatrists
        - Working with patients, carers and their organisation

Exercise Nine

Write a 300-word news story for the Wolverhampton Gazette, using the information contained in the following article, plus any 'made up' information and quotes. Do not forget to get a regional angle in your piece.

22 repossession danger areas revealed by government
The government today revealed 22 areas deemed to be most at risk from repossession.

The 22 areas highlighted are: Barking and Dagenham, Corby, Knowsley, Salford, Newham, Walsall, Redditch, Halton, Sandwell, Wolverhampton, Nottingham, Birmingham, Manchester, Bolton, Liverpool, Sunderland, Reading, Swindon, Northampton, Kingston-upon-Hull, and Cannock Chase.

Data from the Council of Mortgage Lenders show in the second quarter of 2009 2.43 per cent of mortgages were three months of more in arrears.

This represents 270,400 homeowners falling behind with their mortgages.

A total of 11,400 were recorded - but around a quarter these were voluntary possession where homeowners handed back keys to lenders without seeking help to stay in their home.

The admission of the danger areas comes as the government is trying to target help that is on offer to homeowners who are struggling with their mortgages.

The department for Communities and Local Government (CLG) claims over 300,000 people have received help and advice in paying their mortgage since April 2008.

Housing minister John Healey, launching the newspaper, online and billboard adverts today, said: "When homeowners are under pressure and feel their finances are spiralling out of control, the worst thing they can do is bury their heads in the sand.

"I want them to know that sensible, impartial advice is available online or over the phone so they are able to arm themselves with the facts and take control."

A new mortgage advice website for those having financial troubles has also been launched.

Advice is available to those struggling to make payments, all the way to those facing court and repossession.

"In most cases where people seek help they are able to keep their home, so we have made sure a range of support is available to them," Mr Healy said.

He pointed to free debt advice, income support for mortgage interest, agreements from lenders to show greater tolerance and understanding to those in arrears, on-the-day legal advice for those facing court hearings and Mortgage Rescue Scheme for the most vulnerable households.

"The action we've taken means we've seen recent drops in the numbers of repossessions, but there's no room for complacency," the minister added.

"The message of today's campaign is clear: it's your home - let's keep it that way. The adverts will appear across the country, and particularly in those 22 most at risk, to reassure people that they are not alone, and that help is out there at every step of the way."

The key advice is not to ignore the problem and take action, whether taking free debt advice or speaking directly to your lender.

Exercise Ten
This exercise is based on the press release below. Please read it, along with the editors' notes, and write a 150-word article to include the main points and one pertinent quote for an online freight magazine. You have only 30 minutes until deadline. Get writing and time yourself!

Lorry drivers warned by immigration officers
A three week campaign emphasising hauliers' responsibilities in the fight against illegal immigration has been carried out by the UK Border Agency across the midlands and the east of England.

Operation Hedya, which concluded on Friday 31 July, targeted lorry drivers who fail to properly secure their vehicles.

Officers visited lorry drop hotspots - including Clacket Lane services in Surrey, Thurrock and Birchanger services in Essex, South Mimms services in Hertfordshire and Warwick services in

Warwickshire - reminding drivers about the importance of conducting the correct security checks.

Drivers can face heavy financial penalties if they do not secure their lorries properly - more than £68,000 was recovered during the campaign from drivers and companies identified with unpaid civil penalties from previous immigration checks.

Simon Excell, UK Border Agency deputy director, said: "Our top priority is to stop would-be illegal immigrants before they reach the UK. By highlighting to drivers their own responsibilities as well as the potential penalties they face if they do not implement an effective security system we are winning the fight against clandestine entry to the UK.

"We have already seen a significant fall in illegal immigrants sneaking in to the UK thanks to high profile operations like this one and the deployment of a mobile detention van which patrols the motorways of the Midlands and East of England.

"The message is getting out to would-be illegal migrants and organised smuggling gangs that we will catch them, we will detain them and we will deport them."

The operation was led by Immigration Officer Dave Butler, of the Stansted Enforcement Unit, who said: "This operation only strengthens the continued effort to deter clandestine illegal entry and sends a clear message to hauliers."

Notes to editors
1.   All road hauliers travelling to the UK must operate an effective system to prevent the carriage of clandestine entrants. If not, hauliers are subject to a penalty of up to £2,000 per clandestine entrant carried.
2.   The UK Border Agency was launched on 3 April 2008, bringing in a single force to protect our borders, control migration for the benefit of the country, prevent border tax fraud, smuggling and immigration crime and make quick and fair decisions on asylum claims.
3.   Since January this year the UK Border Agency has stopped over 14,000 individual attempts to cross the channel illegally and searched over 400,000 freight vehicles to check they are not harbouring illegal migrants.

Exercise Eleven

1) Pick a topical story from today's news. Look at the Times and how it covers the story. Then get a copy of a tabloid like the Sun and see how it covers the same story. The Sun and the Times, irrespective of their political leanings or reporting style, are exceptionally well written.

2) Pay attention to the opening paragraphs. What are the differences and similarities between each newspaper?

Revision exercise

It is now time for the final exercise of the chapter.

The task for the news writing chapter is simple:
Write a 300-word news story on a topic that interests you. For this exercise make up quotations from fictitious people, or use those from real people. Ensure that you follow all the guidance that we have outlined.

Check your story against this list:
1) Does the introduction include as many of the five Ws and the H as possible?
2) Is the most important point at the top?
3) Does the story unfold logically?
4) Do you have a quotation?
5) Can you cut from the bottom without affecting the sense of the piece?
6) Is it news?
7) Is it to length?
8) Have you checked for grammar, spelling etc?
9) Have you double-checked any facts in the piece including names and titles?

Further reading

Anna McKane, *News Writing*, Sage Publications, 2006

Walter Fox, *Writing the News: A guide for Print Journalists*, Wiley Blackwell, 2001

William David Sloan, *The Great Reporters: An Anthology of News Writing at it Best*, Vision Pr, 1992

McNae's *Essential Law for Journalists*, OUP Oxford

Frances Quinn, *Law for Journalists*, Longman (2007).

THE LANGUAGE OF JOURNALISM

Every year university lecturers, politicians and almost everyone aged over 40, laments the appalling decline in standards of written and spoken English. It has been said for generations but surprisingly we can still write and speak English. These dire predictions about the demise of English are nonsense and have more to do with unwillingness to recognise that English is an evolving language that is still rapidly changing.

That change is because language reflects the values of our time. We live in a much less deferential society and use less formal language than previous generations. This is evident in the way we make less fuss about titles, and use language that is more forthright and more explicit than used as little as twenty years ago. This does not mean that we have abandoned formal spelling and grammar. Such sloppy writing has no place in journalism, or anywhere else, and we make no apology for devoting the third chapter of this course to language and grammar.

Words and sentences are the tools of the journalist's craft, the means by which journalists tell stories and communicate ideas. This chapter is about how you choose and use words and structure them into sentences. But it is more than a basic lesson in grammar and spelling, although this forms much of what you will do. It is about the techniques journalists use to handle language, how we select words and order sentences that make copy come alive.

And the chapter it is also an opportunity for you to practice writing. We start with the basics of spelling and grammar, then explore sentence structure, and finally what makes good writing.

Spelling and grammar

Your spelling must be perfect. Spelling errors indicate poor literacy skills or sloppiness. Neither is acceptable and your copy will be rejected, and rightly so.

If you are poor at spelling, and most people are, make the effort to check words in a dictionary when you are not sure of their spelling. A copy of Webster's, Collins or Oxford dictionaries should be on your desk in addition to the version on your desktop. Most computers include a dictionary but check what edition you have; it may be a US edition.

Do not rely on the spelling check programme of your word processor. These programmes check spelling, not whether you have chosen the right word. They cannot reliably distinguish between the use of 'their' and 'there', tonne and ton, Labour and labour, him and hymn, advise and advice, tenant and tenent, compliment and complement. And if the spell check is set to another language, labor and labour.

The spell check programme is useful. Set it to highlight misspelt words as you type and correct your spelling errors as you see them. Do not rely solely on a quick check at the end: you will not learn to spell and this approach is almost guaranteed to introduce mistakes.

If you repeatedly make the same spelling error try to learn the correct spelling of your problem words: emission with one M, accommodation with two Cs, two Ms and two Os. If you are freelancing in a magazine or newspaper office you may well find your computer – and the freelancer usually gets the oldest one in the office – has no spell check!

Words

The essence of what journalists do is find words to tell a story. Get the words right and everything else including style, sense, and meaning will flow. The skill lies in removing the superfluous words to achieve a balance between economy and accuracy with the right words in the right order. For most people, this means unlearning some bad habits. This chapter will alert you to these and while you may initially still fall into bad habits you should be able to spot them when you proof your copy.

Words must be specific and refer to people. There is no place for the abstract in journalism. Leave that for corporate or government statements where such writing has become an art form. This is writing designed to impress by wordiness and to confuse and obscure meaning. There is no place for phrases like "economy with the truth". If it is a "lie" then say so.

Using multiple words in place of one, like "adverse climatic conditions" instead of "bad weather" or obscure substitutes for commonsense words, like "operative" instead of "worker", or "retail facilities" instead of "shops", and , have no place in journalism.

Pay attention when using verbs as nouns or nouns as verbs, and always use the active form. Instead of "the government will conduct a survey" say "the government will survey". Instead of "the cinema has seating accommodation for 500" say "the cinema seats 500". Misuse of the verb "impact" means it has ost much of the power of its original meaning of forceful collision and is now associated with meaningless business-speak where everything impacts and nothing affects.

Sentences

Sentences carry words ordered to give meaning and tell the story. There are a few rules that can rarely be broken. Every sentence needs a verb, (a doing word, and a subject, a person or thing that is doing). For example: "He hit the policeman". "He" is the subject because he was doing the hitting and "hit" is the verb because that is what he was doing.

The easiest way to check whether you have written a sentence is to ask: "Does it have a subject and a verb?" In this sentence "it" is the subject and "does have" is the verb. If you are a native English speaker it is very likely that you were taught English at school without much formal instruction in grammar. It is more than likely that you use grammar effectively without knowing the rules in a formal way. Familiarity with the language means most people can hear whether a string of words is a sentence or not because it sounds complete when it is: they do not have to stop and think about whether it contains a subject and a verb.

If you find it is not obvious to you, even when you read your work out loud, then you need to get some help with grammar. Join a local class or study a school level English grammar textbook (see Further Reading). You will find it difficult to develop your writing style until you have a good feel sentences.

A sentence is more likely to be easily understood when it is short, expressing one thought or several closely connected ideas. Cramming too many points that are important in their own right into a single sentence may slightly reduce the number of words but will make comprehension and readability more difficult. Consider this sentence:

"Mike Christmas, 42, who until last week worked as a bouncer at the Pussycat nightclub, which has been raided four times by police in the past month, appeared before Dover magistrates yesterday charged with grievous bodily harm, an arrestable offence that carries a fine of up to £5,000 and a maximum prison sentence of five years meaning he will automatically have his case referred to a Crown Court."

This is hard to read and it is unclear what the most important fact is, or what connects the various facts. There are 68 words in that sentence but you do not have to count the words or apply complex formula developed by academics like Rudolf Flesch to realise it is too long and difficult to read.

English Rules OK
Whenever a rule is proclaimed in English you can be sure there is an exception, sometimes several. Treat this as one of the delights of the English language. The exceptions to the rules apply as much to grammar as to spelling and there is nothing that can be done to resolve this other than to learn the exceptions. But the more simple and straightforward your writing, the less likely you are to encounter the exceptions: with certain exceptions of course.

Still confused?
Do not feel overwhelmed by grammar and punctuation. At the end of this chapter, we give you ten simple rules you can apply that will keep you out of trouble, most of the time. Spelling, however, is simply a question of learning, and if you cannot remember how to spell a word or if you have the slightest doubt about spelling, then check.

Readability tests

Rudolph Flesch wrote extensively about the virtue of plain English and created the Flesch-Kincaid readability test. The grammar check software on your computer uses the Flesch formula, or a similar analysis, to calculate readability scores in order to come up with warnings about sentence length. Flesch advocated an average of 18 words per sentence for ease of reading although sentences this short can make copy stilted and appear a little too basic. While this is suitable for readability of official forms, documents and similar material, it is not always appropriate for news and feature article in newspapers and magazines. British newspapers use sentences typically 20 to 25 words long. This is about the maximum but requires skill and practice to perfect.

Writing with nouns and verbs

Good writing is minimalist so avoid unnecessary adjectives. Learn to write with nouns and verbs. Do not write: "The mayor stood to stupendous applause ringing across the upper reaches of the council chamber." All that is required is: "The chamber applauded the mayor."

Enthusiastic use of adjectives rapidly removes objectivity from a story especially when emotional states are attributed to people. "The prime minister angrily dismissed protestors". Can you be sure he was angry, or was he just irritated, or maybe he was frightened?

What you think of as extraordinary noun and adjective combinations are clichéd: get rid of the adjective and choose a better noun.

Avoid using words to modify adjectives that are absolutes. Adjectives like absolute, certain, complete, devoid, empty, entire, essential, eternal, everlasting, fatal, perfect, pure, worthless, ultimate, untouchable, cannot and should not be modified. Avoid meaningless modifiers like real danger, final outcome, or unduly alarmed.

Exercise 1

Take the sentence below and write each idea as a single sentence. You will need at least 6 sentences. Check your answer against the one we provide at the end of the chapter, but no cheating and looking first!

"Mike Christmas, 42, who until last week worked as a bouncer at the Pussycat nightclub, which has been raided four times by police in the past month, appeared before Dover magistrates yesterday charged with grievous bodily harm, an arrestable offence that carries a fine of up to £5,000 and a maximum prison sentence of five years meaning he will automatically have his case referred to a Crown Court."

Exercise 2

The story below is from the Guardian newspaper but originally written in four sentences. Re-write the story using four sentences. There is no need to change the order of the words or the sentences. Simply place full stops where appropriate and add a few extra words to get four sentences that make the piece easier to read and understand.

"Gordon Brown today said he wanted MPs to vote to abolish their controversial second home allowance next week saying parliament needed immediate reform of the MPs' expenses system because voters had "lost confidence" in the way it operated. The announcement marks a significant U-turn by Brown, who until today had resisted calls from David Cameron and Nick Clegg for reforms of MPs' expenses to be introduced quickly, arguing that parliament should wait until the committee on standards in public life had completed its inquiry into the matter."

Sentence structure

Keeping your sentence structure simple not only makes for snappy copy but also avoids the many and varied pitfalls that come with complex sentence construction.

Essentially there are four types of sentence: simple, compound, complex and complex compound. Using nothing but simple sentences produces very stilted copy with repetitious phrasing. Joining sentences to create compound sentences and adding phrases, or clauses to qualify and enhance meaning, makes complex and complex-compound sentences, like this one, that can be hard to read.

The following illustrates the structure:
Simple sentence: *Yesterday eight men robbed a bank.*
Simple sentence: *Robbers stole £10,000 from a bank.*

Join the two together with a conjunction, "and" to produce a compound sentence: *Yesterday eight men robbed a bank and stole £10,000*

Introduce a phrase and you create a complex sentence:
Yesterday eight men wearing balaclavas and carrying machine guns robbed a bank. The phrase "wearing balaclavas and carrying machine guns" is a subordinate statement modifying the main statement.

Compound complex sentence:
Eight men wearing balaclavas and carrying machine guns who robbed a bank yesterday were arrested when their get-away van broke down outside the bank.

This sentence illustrates the basic structure of sentences and is not an example of good news writing. It does highlight the danger when the complex sentence tries to carry too many ideas that confuse the reader.

Take this overly complex sentence for example:
Tamil Tiger rebels fighting government forces in northeast Sri Lanka who have declared a unilateral ceasefire have been beaten back to a 5sq m area where the UN says some 50,000 civilians remain trapped but the army puts the number at 15,000.

There are fives elements to this story:

- Tamil Tiger rebels are fighting government forces in northeast Sri Lanka
- Tamil Tiger rebels have declared a unilateral ceasefire
- The rebels have been beaten back to a 5sq m area
- The UN says some 50,000 civilians remain trapped
- The army puts the number at 15,000.

The first and last two sentences can be combined to read:

Tamil Tiger rebels fighting government forces in northeast Sri Lanka have declared a unilateral ceasefire. The rebels have been beaten back to a 5 sq m area. The UN says some 50,000 civilians remain trapped but the army puts the number at 15,000.

The clause, "fighting government forces in north-east Sri Lanka" has been used as a subordinate clause to allow the first two simple sentences to be combined while the conjunction 'but' joins the last two simple sentences. The statement giving the size of the land area where the rebels are fighting is best left as an idea on its own rather than merged with the disputed number of civilians trapped. A clue here is the length of sentence. To combine the information about the size of the area and the numbers trapped would require a 30 or so word sentence.

Using sentences

A sentence is a self-contained unit of meaning. A news story or an article is constructed by putting these units of meaning in sequence. Meaning should flow from one sentence to the next, carrying the story forward and so telling the story.

If you fail to use proper sentences, or you make them too complicated, the meaning becomes unclear and the reader cannot follow the story. Once the flow of meaning is interrupted you are forcing the reader to try and understand your meaning and they will lose interest.

We need to understand and practice using simple sentences but it would be absurd to suggest that you should limit your writing to simple sentences. We also need to consider sentence structures that are more complex but always remembering the need to limit the sentence to one, or at most a few closely related, ideas.

Exercise 3

The danger comes when we combine sentences unnecessarily into one long sentence, or when we combined sentences carrying different ideas. The 78-word sentence below, does exactly this and is better written in at least three sentences. Your task is re-write the sentence into at least three sentences. But don't get carried away, just create sentences, the order of words in this case can be remain the same.

An investigation carried out by The Sunday Independent has uncovered an incredibly lax attitude towards the sale a new 'over the counter' diet pill by Irish chemists that are selling it to healthy thin young girls despite reassurance by the drug's manufacturer, GlaxoSmithKline that all pharmacists will be trained to calculate a person's Body Mass Index, which must be over 28, and ask buyers suitable "fielding" questions on their motivation for taking the drug before selling the pill.

Order your words carefully

In the exercise above the order of words could be left unchanged. But the danger with a complex compound sentence is getting the order wrong, with subsidiary clauses or phrases appearing ahead of the main idea. Take this example:

Saying that while he accepted the doctor's evidence that the patient had died from a stroke, the death of Michael Watson, a long term resident at Murryfield Care Home, the coroner, Antony Holmes, believed it was more likely to have resulted from neglect.

The reader must read the entire sentence, then start again to establish who 'he' is and what 'he' said about what. The sentence is far better expressed:

The coroner, Antony Holmes, accepted the doctor's evidence that Michael Watson, a long term resident at Murryfield Care Home, had died from a stroke but believed his death was more likely to have resulted from neglect.

Not only is the sentence shorter by seven words but the reader is also immediately clear as to who said what about who. If in doubt remember that it is usually best to start with the person doing the saying: who said what, when, where and why. But not all in one sentence.

Keeping sentences short does not mean your copy should be monotonous. Sentences should vary in length and can be as short as five words and as long as 30. Short sentences create a sense of urgency appropriate in a news story whereas a feature, with more analytical comment, may benefit from longer sentences, which can help vary the pace of the article

There is no rule about sentence length or a formula to apply because this is the mystery and art of writing. Does it have a place in journalism? Yes, but it takes great skill and years of practice. Do not expect literary gems to flow from your keyboard after four weeks. Instead aim for clarity. A good workmanlike writing style is better than failed attempts at literary genius.

Until you are a more experienced writer, and that takes several years, write short, simple sentences that carry your meaning forward a step at a time. Make one point in each sentence. If in doubt and a sentence delivers two points, consider splitting it in two. Our aim in this course is to get you writing good workmanlike prose. Once you have mastered that, you can evolve a more distinctive personal writing style.

The importance of punctuation

Punctuation signals how the grammar of the sentence is supposed to work to ensure that the words are correctly understood. The rules are fairly straightforward and the best advice is to use punctuation marks sparingly. The rule, if in doubt leave it out, will stand you in good stead.

Capitals

A capital letter is used at the start of a sentence and on proper nouns. The Victorians were great enthusiasts for using capitals on almost every noun, a practice that government and business carry on as enthusiastically today. Job titles and job descriptions do not need capitals so limit capitals to people and place names.

Take care with geographic areas like east Yorkshire as distinct from North Yorkshire, West Yorkshire and South Yorkshire that are counties. There is no capital in yorkshire pudding and yorkshire terrier, and no capital for southwest and southeast and all other points of the compass.

Commas

Commas mark sub-sections of a sentence, like phrases and clauses. Used after a job title a comma indicates that there is only one person with this title. For example the comma in the sentence, "The president, Michael Jones, announced huge losses" indicates there is only one president whereas, "The secretary Mary Day added up the numbers incorrectly," denotes more than one secretary.

Unnecessary commas can significantly alter meaning, as with "He is not a hard, pressed person." Likewise with the sentence, "He waited for a red, double deck, bus." He waited for a bus, not especially for one that was also red and with two decks.

Commas should not be used to insert pauses that may be necessary when reading copy out loud. We write in order to be read quietly.

Colons and semicolons

These are frequently used incorrectly largely because many think, wrongly, they are interchangeable. A colon is used, rather than a comma, to introduce a quotation.

As the mayor left the stage he said: "What a dreadful speech." However, there is a strong case that the colon is unnecessary given that the quotation mark introduced the quote. It is entirely acceptable to leave our the colon.

Colons are also used to introduce a list. *Three things are needed for a good speech: eloquence, voice, and confidence.*

A colon should be used between two sentences or parts of a sentence when the first introduces a proposition resolved by the second. *"I'll tell you what I'm going to do: I'm going to quit."*

A semicolon marks a pause which has more emphasis than a comma but less than a full stop. Think of it as a comma and you are less likely to go wrong using it. Some people are brilliant using semicolons; others are less so.

Brackets and dashes

Brackets are rarely needed and best avoided. They are used, like dashes, to separate a statement from a sentence. A dash is not to be confused with a hyphen. The dash, –, is twice as long. Square brackets, (*not* round brackets called parentheses) are used within quoted direct speech to provide essential information to make sense of the quote.

Hyphens

The hyphen is used to link words together as in London black-cab driver where the black refers to the colour of the vehicle and not the driver. If in doubt, use one word rather than hyphenate. Many words begin life as hyphenated words and with usage soon lose the hyphen; words like wire-less, down-stairs. Why wait, use laptop, printout, and the rest without the hyphen. There is little merit in using hyphens that can become clumsy when type is set over narrow measures. Hyphens are not required with compound adjectives where meaning is clear, like civil rights movement. But short compound adjectives do need the hyphen, as with ten-tonne truck, six-year old child or where there is potential for confusion like black-cab driver.

Apostrophes

For some reason people feel the need to insert an apostrophe whenever they see a word ending with s. Resist this temptation. There two places where you use an apostrophe:

1) to determine possession and show that something belongs to something or somebody without using the word 'of'
2) to indicate that words or letters are missing. Note that there is nothing missing from decades such as 1980s or 90s, so they do not use an apostrophe.

There is a simple test to establish whether you need an apostrophe. In the case of possession, see if you can use the word of instead of the apostrophe. If you cannot then you probably do not need it. For example, "My friends' house" means the "The house of my friends". The same technique can be applied to contractions where the apostrophe indicates missing letters. It's or Its? Simply read it in full. If the sentence requires "it is" then it's needs the apostrophe.

Where the word that requires the apostrophe already ends with s then only the apostrophe is added, so its is James' new book not James's new book which is hard to pronounce. Plurals without an s such as men and children take the apostrophe with an s, so write men's magazines, children's games.

Apostrophes are important in that they determine exact meaning. For example:

My brother's friend's cars   one brother, one friend with several cars

My brother's friends' cars	one brother, several friends with cars
My brothers' friends' cars	several brothers, several friends with cars
My brothers' friend's cars	several brothers, one friend with cars

Be careful with expressions of time. An apostrophe is needed for "it will done in three days' time" (ie, the time of three days) but not when expressed, as "it will be done in three days".

Despite the earlier comment about exact meaning, it is rare for a sentence to suffer because an apostrophe has been left out. Stays with the rule, if in doubt leave it out.

Quotation marks

Use double quotes at the beginning and end of the quote with single quote marks to denote quoted words within the quote. All punctuation is placed within the quote where a complete sentence is quoted. The witness said: "I looked out of the window and saw the flames. 'Fire' I shouted, but it was too late." When quoting a few words the punctuation is outside the quote. The witness, observing the flames shouted "Fire", but to no avail.

Exclamation marks

Very, very, rarely – and so rarely we cannot find an example – will you need to use an exclamation mark in your copy. So rarely are they used that the traditional typewriter does not have a key for an exclamation mark. It is created with two key stokes: a single quote with a full stop underneath.

Plurals

Corporate speak likes to pluralise and at the same time speak with a single voice. A company is a single entity so refer to companies in the singular. Nor do companies speak, they have spokespeople who make and issue statements expressing a corporate view, but it is the spokesperson who speaks, not the company.

Accents

Accents are infrequent in English but take care with the spelling of foreign names where they are common. This can be problematic if you submit copy as a text file you should alert the sub edit at first use of the name as to where accents should go. Anglicised French words like cafe do not require an accent but résumé and exposé do in order to distinguish them from existing English words. Cliché is spelt with and without these days. The test is whether there is another English word that could be confused with a word without the accent, like the verbs resume and expose.

Punctuation and quotation marks

The use of quotes marks and punctuation is a source of much argument among grammar pedants. The American and British styles are opposites - the traditional British style is for single quotes with punctuation outside the quote marks. But the differences are more blurred now. Here's a simple guide that mixes both. It is more style than rule that determines usage but whatever style you adopt for quotations, and the method of punctuation you use, be consistent and stick with it. However, when submitting copy to a magazine or web site check to see its house style and follow that.

Easy guide to punctuation with quotations

1 Use a pair double quotes to distinguish the quote - the words of someone other than the writer (you).
Michael Jones, speaking after the incident, said "I was gob smacked."
Note that there is no comma, semi colon of colon before the first quote mark and the end full stop is within the quote.

2 A quotation is set off by quotation marks and nothing else. A sentence containing a quotation is punctuated exactly like any other sentence apart from the addition of the quotation marks. You should not insert additional punctuation marks into the sentence merely to warn the reader that a quotation is coming up: that's what the quotation marks are for. However, if the quote is acting as an explanation then a colon is used to indicate this. *John Jones has one golden rule for sales: "The customer is always right."*

3 If the speaker is also quoting then use single quote marks to denote the quote within the quote. *Inspector Jones said "The defendant was in a highly shocked state and kept repeating 'I was gob smacked' when we questioned him."*

4 If you must interrupt the quote, and it is generally unnecessary, then you need a second set of quotes and more punctuation. *"The only tiger I like", said William Blake "is a stuffed tiger."*

5 Keep things simple. Rewrite your sentence if trying to use a quote requires all sorts of devices and explanation. Occasionally you may find it necessary to interrupt a quotation you are citing in order to clarify something (the name of a person for example. To do this you enclose your remarks in square brackets (never parentheses - round brackets). *According to Michael Jones, "He [Arthur Waddington] had never placed a bet in his life."*

6 If you want to quote parts of a speech or passage while leaving out some intervening bits, you do this by inserting a suspension (...) also called ellipses, to represent a missing section of a quotation. If, as a result, you need to provide one or two extra words to link up the pieces

of the quotation, you put those extra words inside square brackets to show that they are not part of the quotation. *Speaking to delegates Harry Balls said "[local] business leaders must recognise... the implication of the new legislation."*

But if you need to add more and more missing words and suspensions is probably better not to quote and paraphrase into a simple sentence.

7 Huge argument ranges over the problem of whether to put other punctuation marks inside or outside the quotation marks. It makes sense that the only punctuation marks placed inside the quotation marks are those that form part of the quotation, while all others should be placed outside. *Shakespeare's play Richard III contains the line "Now is the winter of our discontent".*

There is no full stop inside the quote because the line from play does not have one. The full quote reads, *Now is the winter of our discontent/ Made glorious summer by this sun of York*. Note the use of the slash to denote line breaks in poetry.

What makes good writing

Good writing is concise, exactly balancing economy of words with communicating ideas. It is lively, stimulating and above all easy to read. Good writing is universal, applying to academic texts as much as to newspaper articles. To write well requires practice and study and is like playing a musical instrument. It is not a god-given gift but a skill that must be developed. There are some elementary techniques that must be applied. These are described below but you will need to practice these by completing the exercises and assignments, to hone your skills as a good writer.

Active not passive

If there is one golden rule it must be to write in the active voice. Despite being easier to write an active sentence most people default to the passive. Active sentences are easier to read and use fewer words. The grammar check on your computer is a huge aid highlighting the passive voice. But save yourself a lot of editing and write in the active in the first place.

Consider these few examples:

Police arrested the minister. The subject, police, is the actor and the minister is the object. Turn the sentence round so minister is the subject and you get the passive, The minister was arrested by police.

A meeting will be held by the local council next week. It is far better to say, "The local council will hold a meeting next week'.

There are times when you need to use the passive voice. A news story about the prime minister usually calls for him or her to be the subject as in "The prime minister was found guilty by the High Court. "

Be especially aware that company statements and official documents are usually written in the passive voice. Expect to read copy like, The board of directors has been made aware of complaints about rudeness by staff and has forwarded these to the customer services division. You need to write, The customer service division will deal with complaints made to the board about rude staff.

Be Positive

Newspapers do the telling which is best done with positive statements even if you are expressing a negative. Instead of:

- "The new road scheme was not successful"
write "The new road scheme failed".
- "The bank robbers have not been caught"
write "The bank robbers are still at large".
- "The directors did not respond to the complaints"
write "The directors ignored the complaints".

Beware the double negative as in "It is unlikely that bank rates will not be raised". What you are trying to say is, "It is likely that bank rates will be raised". So say it!

Tenses and reported speech

Direct speech is accurate and lively but rarely can an entire article be constructed solely of direct speech. For reasons of economy, and to avoid boredom, you need to revert to reported speech. But be ruthless when you do. Do not try to include all the wordiness, pauses, laughs or verbosity of the speaker. Do not adopt the language of the speaker and include his or her nonsense like "fitness for purpose", "interface with stakeholders", "pleased to say", "cannot be denied", or "this moment in time". Your job is to render into intelligible English in as few words as possible what the speaker was saying.

Tenses can cause all sorts of problems with reported speech. Use the past tense when reporting speech. The driver said: "I like fast cars" in reported speech is written as "The driver liked fast cars", not "The driver said he likes fast cars". If the comment was made in the past tense, and the driver said: "I liked fast cars" then this is written as: "The driver said he had liked fast cars".

Once you have established who is speaking continue with the past tense. And be consistent with tenses, start mixing them and all sorts of problems develop.

Using a Thesaurus

Simple words are generally better than long words. English does have an enormous vocabulary and while there are some subtle variations in meanings it is rare that you need these, so be cautious when looking up new words in a Thesaurus.

There are occasions where, in order to avoid repetition of words that starts to become clumsy, some alternatives are needed. A story about industrial action could refer to a strike, dispute, quarrel, disagreement, or altercation, but exercise restraint as too many words, or using obscure words, will confuse the reader. Take the word efficacious, meaning to have beneficial effect. Appropriate in a Victorian discussion about herbal remedies but not in a news story about the latest medical treatments.

Take great care to avoid inventing or finding ever more nouns to avoid repetition. There is nothing wrong with saying he or she when you have mentioned someone. The same applies with organisations with long names reduced to meaningless acronyms. For example, in a story mentioning the Society of British Water and Wastewater Industries where the abbreviation SBWWI is almost meaningless and clumsy, subsequent references should be to "the society".

And there is nothing wrong with repeating the words say or said after or before a quote. It is far better to repeat said or say than to become ever more inventive with pointed out, expressed, opined, observed, stated, explained, reported, shouted, continued, added, declared, and the list goes on. Never substitute admit for say: the implication is that the statement has been unwillingly made. Likewise with claimed which implies doubt about accuracy or truthfulness.

Ten steps to improve grammar and punctuation

If you feel you are never going to master the rules of grammar and punctuation fear not. If you keep your sentences short and follow these basic rules shown below you will not go far wrong. Journalism is not literature, it's about telling a story, usually short and fast , so that the clipped style characterised by short sentences works well.

Simple Punctuation Rules

1   Start the sentence with a capital letter and end with a full stop
2   Use commas sparingly, no more than two in a sentence
3   Use colons only to introduce a list
4   Do NOT use semi colons or exclamation marks
5   Use a question mark only in a quoted question, never your text
6   If in doubt about using an apostrophe leave it out

Simple Grammar Rules

7   Keep your sentences short
8   Start the sentence with what is important then follow with the action, that is the verb
9   Do not use verbs that end in ing - such as walking, shooting, crying.
Use the active: walked, shot, cried.
10 Forget descriptive words, the adjectives, such as boldly, carefully, happily. When used badly, which is more often than not, they turn good copy into flowery prose

Exercise 5

This exercise is a little harder and requires that you apply much of what you learned in this chapter. The following story appeared on a web site. Re-write the story applying the good writing practices described in this chapter.

To help, follow these steps:

1) Split any long sentences into shorter sentences with one idea per sentence

2) Change sentences from passive to active where possible

2) Arrange the sentences into order with those containing the most important ideas first

3) keep the language simple

4) write the story in full. Now consider joining any sentences to improve flow and readability

Royal Dutch Shell today posted profits of $3.3bn (£2.26bn) for the first three months of 2009, down 58% on a year earlier. The Anglo-Dutch firm made profits of £22bn last year, but, in line with BP yesterday, it said the weaker global economy had impacted its performance.

As well as oil prices below $50 a barrel, having peaked at $147 in July, Shell has been affected by security concerns in Nigeria, OPEC quota restrictions and weakening industrial demand for gas.

Chief Executive Jeroen van der Veer said the company continued to make 'significant investments' in order to maintain future profitability.

He added: 'Industry conditions remain challenging, and our focus is on capital discipline and costs. We are taking a prudent approach to this downturn, focused on sustaining a strong position in the energy landscape.'

Today's figures were ahead of market expectations, with profits before exceptionals of $2.96bn (£2.03bn) well ahead of the $2.6bn (£1.78bn) forecast in the City.

BP reported a sharp drop in profits yesterday, with its first-quarter haul falling 62% to $2.39bn (£1.64bn). This figure was also stronger than City forecasts.

Steep profit falls are also expected later this week from US companies ExxonMobil and Chevron.

Shell pledged earlier this year to maintain net investment at near to last year's level of $32bn (£21.9bn) in order to safeguard future profitability.

The company has moved into more expensive areas of production such as tar sands.

Ten easy steps to good writing

Good writing is concise, exactly balancing economy of words with communicating ideas. It is lively, stimulating, and above all easy to read. Good writing is universal, applying to academic texts as much as to newspaper articles or business reports. Good writing is a skill not an art. It is about telling a story concisely and accurately. Good writing follows a basic formula that anyone can apply Here's how...

1 Have a structure

Like all good fairy tales, what you write should have a beginning, middle, and an end. You also need a theme; what journalists call an angle. Everything that goes into the article must conform to a hierarchy. That is, the ideas and information are all ordered in terms of importance. When you plan your writing, and planning is the key to good writing, top-load the essential and most interesting elements of the story with supporting information following in order of diminishing importance. This structure ensures that that you present the most important facts first, rather than requiring the reader to go through several paragraphs to find them. It enables readers to stop reading at any point and still come away with the essence of a story.

2 Use a strong opening

Your objective when writing is to impart information, facts, or opinion: so tell people what they need to know starting with the most important first. Your opening sentence should grab the reader's attention. It needs to be focused, short, and memorable. That first sentence is like the headline of a newspaper article: it needs to summarise the story. It is the first and possibly only chance you have of getting the reader's attention and persuading them to carry on reading.

3 Amplify the opening

Your second paragraph is where you expand on what you have said in those first few opening sentences. Here you add a little detail with a few more facts to entice the reader to paragraph three.

4 Now say why it's important

The third paragraph provides the context of what you are saying and tells the reader why the information is important. By now, the reader is hooked and you can safely move onto the subsequent paragraphs to expand and develop the story.

5 Build the detail

After the introduction, the rest of the article explains and expands on the beginning, giving the reader more information in order of decreasing importance. Subsequent paragraphs add more information, facts, and opinions depending on your subject matter. But keep the ideas grouped together, do not take the reader down a labyrinth and hope they will be able to make sense of what you say.

6 Wrap it up

Unless you are writing a short item like a news story for a newsletter or similar, then wrap the article with a concluding paragraph that links to the opening paragraph. This can be as simple as a restatement in one sentence of the opening idea or a more sophisticated conclusion in a paragraph or two that restates the main theme of the article. The conclusion is a reminder to the reader of that opening sentence. It should never contain any new information.

7 Kill the purple prose

Your aim when writing is to inform, persuade, or educate. You are not writing literature so do not use lots of heavily descriptive language. Keep your sentences and paragraphs short. If you find sentences littered with commas, stretching out to include clauses and sub clauses, then it is probably time to stop and begin a new sentence. When you have finished, go through the article or report and remove any words that are not completely necessary. These are usually adjectives, get rid of them and stick to the facts; it will read far better.

8 Be active not passive

The default writing style for most people is passive, characterised by using verbs that end in "ing". For example, he was walking, instead of he walked, the company was buying instead of the company bought.

Keep the writing active, seize those verbs, and make them work for you, not trailing behind a stream of multi-syllabic nouns or adjectives. Instead of "the department will conduct a survey" say, "the department will survey". Instead of "the cinema has seating accommodation for 500" say "the cinema seats 500". You will be amazed at how much livelier your writing becomes simply by using active language.

9 Say what you mean

Get straight to the point and say what you mean. Use short, snappy, precise words. Avoid foreign words, jargon, and use technical words only when your audience is familiar with them. Aim to write technical material so that anyone can understand it. Do not use abbreviations that can mystify your readers. Avoid slang that diminishes the value of your writing and makes it less credible.

Words must be specific. Using multiple words in place of one, like "adverse climatic conditions" instead of "bad weather" or obscure substitutes for commonsense words, like "operative" instead of "worker", or "retail facilities" instead of "shops", and "enhanced interrogation technique" instead or "torture", have no place in good writing.

Sentences carry words ordered to give meaning. Meaning should flow from one sentence to the next, carrying the story forward, and so telling the story. A sentence is more easily understood when it is short, expressing one thought or several closely connected ideas. Cramming too many points that are important in their own right into a single sentence may slightly reduce the number of words but will make comprehension and readability more difficult. Sentences, which should rarely exceed 25 words, are like the complete article and should have the most important facts at the beginning.

Consider this example: *Having walked the marathon route twice, George was able to plan his timing easily*. It is the second part that interests us, so start with it: *George planned his timing easily by walking the marathon twice.*

Similarly when making comparisons using 'like' and 'as'. Never start a sentence with these two words. Instead of: *As with good writing, good history requires precision with words*, write: *Good writing, like good history, requires precision with words.*

10 Make no spelling mistakes

Your spelling and grammar must be perfect. Spelling errors indicate poor literacy skills or sloppiness and undermine the value of what you are saying. If you are poor at spelling, and most people are, make the effort to check words in a dictionary when you are not sure of their spelling. A dictionary should be on your desk in addition to the version on your desktop.

Do not rely on the spelling check programme of your word processor. These programmes check spelling, not whether you have chosen the right word and cannot reliably distinguish between the use of 'their' and 'there', tonne and ton, Labour and labour, him and hymn, advise and advice, tenant and tenet, compliment and complement.

Answers to the exercises

Answer Exercise 1
Mike Christmas is 42 years old.
He worked as a bouncer at the Pussycat nightclub until last week.
Police raided the Pussycat Nightclub four times in the past month.
Yesterday, Mike Christmas appeared before Dover magistrates charged with grievous bodily harm.
Grievous bodily harm is an arrestable offence that carries a fine of up to £5,000 and a maximum prison sentence of five years.
Due to the high sentence and fine grievous bodily harm cases cannot be heard in a Magistrates Court and must be referred to a Crown Court.

Answer Exercise 2
Gordon Brown today said he wanted MPs to vote to abolish their controversial second home allowance next week. The prime minister said parliament needed immediate reform of the MPs' expenses system because voters had "lost confidence" in the way it operated. The announcement marks a significant U-turn by Brown, who until today had resisted calls from David Cameron and Nick Clegg for reforms of MPs' expenses to be introduced quickly. The prime minister had argued that parliament should wait until the committee on standards in public life had completed its inquiry into the matter.

Answer Exercise 3
Mike Christmas, a 42-year old former nightclub bouncer, appeared before Dover magistrates charged with grievous bodily harm. Christmas previously worked at the Pussycat nightclub, which police have raided four times in the past month. The case against Christmas will be referred to a Crown Court because the offence carries a fine of up to £5,000 and a maximum prison sentence of five years, sentences greater than magistrates are able to impose.

Answer Exercise 4
Irish chemists have an incredibly lax attitude towards the sale of a new 'over the counter' diet pill. An investigation carried out by the *Sunday Independent* has uncovered chemists willing to sell the drug to healthy thin young girls despite reassurance by the drug's manufacturer,

GlaxoSmithKline. It claims that all pharmacists will be trained to calculate a person's Body Mass Index, which must be over 28, and ask buyers suitable "fielding" questions on their motivation for taking the drug before selling the pill.

Answer to Exercise 5
There is no right answer; this is one possible version.
Royal Dutch Shell today posted profits of £2.26bn ($3.3bn) for the first three months of 2009, down 58% on the previous year when it reported a £22bn profit. Today's figures were ahead of market expectations, with profits before exceptionals of £2.03bn ($2.96bn) ahead of the £1.78bn ($2.6bn) City forecast.

Chief executive, Jeroen van der Veer, said: "Industry conditions remain challenging, and our focus is on capital discipline and costs. We are taking a prudent approach to this downturn, focused on sustaining a strong position in the energy landscape."

He said Shell continued to make "significant investments" in line with its pledge earlier this year to maintain net investment at near to last year's level of £21.9bn ($32bn) in order to safeguard future profitability.

Shell blamed the poor performance on a weak global economy. It has also been affected by security concerns in Nigeria, Opec quota restrictions, weakening industrial demand for gas, and oil prices below $50 a barrel, well below the peak of $147 in July. The company has moved into more expensive areas of production such as tar sands.

Shell's performance is in line with BP which yesterday reported it first quarter profits falling 62% to £1.64bn ($2.39bn) because of weak global demand but better than City forecasts.

US companies Exxon Mobil and Chevron are expected to report similar profit falls later this week.

GLOSSARY A - Z A list of common confusions and errors

adrenaline a hormone that increases heart rate and blood pressure not to be confused with Adrenalin, trademark and brand name for a drug containing adrenaline

affect and effect are the source of much confusion. Both words can be used as a verb or noun but affect as a noun is limited to psychology meaning emotion or desire and especially in the context of influencing behaviour as in 'she affected sympathy with those who lost their jobs'. Affect as a verb as in "smoking during pregnancy can affect a baby's development. Effect as a verb as in "I hope to effect a change in your spelling"

aggravate to make worse not to annoy

alternative is often confused with **choice**. There are only ever two alternatives whereas you have many choices

among means to share. "The syndicate shared the Lottery winnings among themselves with nothing given to any charity." Do not use where you mean between, as in "The dispute between British banks led to the problem." Use among not amongst, which is old fashioned. This also applies to whilst and amidst

amok not amuck

antenna a pair of sensory appendages found on insects or a radio aerial. The plural for insects is **antennae**, for radios it is **antennas**

anticipate is to take action in expectation of something, not to expect it

appraise is to evaluate whereas **apprise** is to inform

arguable and **beleaguered** overused so avoid

as or since? As indicates consequence. I cannot submit my assignment as the Internet is down' whereas since indicates time, 'I have not heard from the editor since I last telephoned'

aspirin a synthetic compound used to relieve mild pain not to be confused with Disprin, the trademark and brand name for a product containing aspirin. Beware the many other band names that need a capital letter. Blu-Tack is a trademark as are Sellotape, Hoover, Portakabin, Google and Durex so use capitals but not for cellophane which used to be a trademark but became so widely used to describe clear plastic film it lost it trademark status following a court ruling

auger, used to make holes, unlike **augur** which is to predict

average is the same as **mean** but different to **median** For example, consider wages in a company. Average is used to express Mean, which is the sum of the wages divided by the number of people. This is not the same number as the Median which is the point below which half of all employees earn less or more when you line up everyone's wages from lowest to highest. If doing the calculations yourself remember that you cannot average an average. If the drivers' average wage is £10 and that for clerks is £20, the average wage of clerks and drivers is not £15. You have to add all drivers' and all clerks' wages then divide by the total number of people to establish the average for both groups together

baby seal is an example of language as propaganda where the word carries implicit meaning. Would you write baby sheep instead of lambs? Like dogs, the young of seals are called pups

begs the question best avoided as it is usually misused. It does not mean to ask a question but to assume a proposition that carries a conclusion

bellwether (not weather) is a sheep with a bell on its neck that leads the flock. The term is used to signal something that sets an example as in "Since 1923 Dover has been a bellwether constituency" meaning that the party that wins the seat in a general election forms the government

bid, acceptable only in financial reporting as in a company bid to buy another

billion, abbreviated as lower case bn as in £10bn (unlike million which is abbreviated as "m"). The American valuation of 1,000 million is generally accepted. Since the credit crunch a trillion, abbreviated at lower case tn, has entered the vocabulary which is a million million. British usage, now rare, valued a billion as a million million and a trillion as a million million million

big is the way to describe these numbers. Avoid major, massive, mammoth, giant, etc

Britain is the same as the **United Kingdom** and includes England, Scotland, Wales and Northern Ireland. Great Britain is a geographic term that includes England, Wales and Scotland but not the island of Ireland. Take care when talking about Britain and British that you mean Britain and not England and Wales. This is especially important in the context of acts of parliament, legislation and government agencies. The Environment Agency for example functions in England and Wales.

Its equivalent in Scotland is the Scottish Environmental Protection Agency while Northern Ireland has its own department. Scotland is a country in its own right with a separate legal system, separate education system, and its own parliament; similarly with Northern Ireland. See Ulster below for confusion about Northern Ireland.

but and **however** are overused, often incorrectly as conjunctions to link statement that agree. "I like eggs but not bacon" not "I like eggs but also bacon". A quick guide it to substitute "however" for "but" and see if the sentence still reads correctly

canon and **cannon**. A canon is a cleric or decree or type of music. Cannons are guns that you fire

canvas and **canvass**. Canvas makes a tent for camping. The verb to canvass is what politicians do prior to elections

claimed implies deceit. Avoid and use said

commented, said is preferable. Avoid exclaimed, expressed, opined and the myriad other similar words

compare to and **compare with**. When you compare to, it is a likeness that is suggested as in "Shall I compare you to a summers' day?" If you compare with, it is a comparison, as in "To see the difference in news writing compare the Guardian with the Dover Echo

compliment and **complement** You write beautifully is to compliment whereas your beautiful writing complements your excellent research skill means to add to

comprise, Britain comprises many nationalities . As with the words contains and includes, there is no "of"

crescendo is a passage of music that steadily increases in volume which then reaches a climax. You cannot rise to a crescendo

disk and **disc**. Now interchangeable despite the efforts of purists. Disk, the US spelling was used with computer teminology and disc the British spelling with anything other than computers

dependant is the person who relies on someone else and is therefore **dependent** on that person

dilemma is not the same as a problem, it is being faced with a choice of action

discomfit, a verb, is to make someone uneasy whereas **discomfort**, a noun, is to feel uneasy

drug use A few scientists might experiment with drugs but most people use them. Say what you mean, do not use language designed to obfuscate

enervate is to weaken and quite the opposite of **energise** which is to invigorate

exotic means foreign not glamorous like some weeds which are exotic plants but ugly

fewer is used when items are indivisible like people (you can count them), **less** is used with infinitely divisible materials like water. "We need less sand because we have fewer bricks to lay."

flaunt means to show off, parade and display unlike **flout** which means to mock and abuse

Kashmir is the place whereas **cashmere** is the expensive fabric obtained from the wool of the cashmere goat

licence is the noun and **license** with the s is the verb

literally means exactly like. There is no case of anyone literally exploding with anger

luxurious is something full of luxury but **luxuriant** is to produce abundantly. Cars are luxurious, flowers luxuriant

mitigate means to appease or soften whereas **militate**, which sounds like military, means to make war

practice is the noun but **practise** with an S is the verb. "In order to practise medicine the doctor needed a practice"

principal is the first in rank, like the principal of a school but **principle** is a moral conviction

print when used as a verb does not need out attached to. Printout as a noun is now widely used.

protagonists and **antagonists** are not opposites. The protagonist is the leading character in a play, book or film. An antagonist is someone who actively opposes

questions should never be asked of the reader. Your job is to inform readers not interrogate them

stationery and **stationary** stationery, a noun, with the E is the paper on which we print our E-mails while stationary, an adjective, with the A is what happens to cars during a traffic jam

ships and yachts are objects. It ran aground, not she

stalemate as all chess players know is the end of the game. The word you probably want is **deadlock** or **impasse**

tax avoidance and **evasion** are very different; avoidance is legal, evasion is criminal

terrorist and **terrorism** are highly politicised terms. As journalists we are striving for objectivity and labels like terrorist are subjective. Nelson Mandela before his election as president was a "freedom fighter" feted throughout the world but branded a "terrorist" by the South African government. Whatever label you use endeavour to remain neutral

that appearing after "said" can often be deleted to improve sentence flow

the can be a troublesome word but do not leave it out as in "conference said" or "government did" which sounds like the jargon such organisations encourage. In the case of names of newspaper and pubs like the *Times*, the *Guardian*, the *Coach and Horses*, use a low case t. Book titles retain the capital

titles Baroness, barons, are referred to as Lord or Lady with their surname without first name so it is Lady Thatcher not Lady Margaret Thatcher

trademarks are identified with a capital letter, but only the first letter not the entire word. Companies are highly protective about their trademarks and will take action when they are abused. And it does not make for happy editors if you land their publication in a lawsuit. Some brands are so well known it is easy to assume they are a generic name. And it is a peculiarly British habit to take brand names and reduce them to generics, like Biro for a ballpoint pen, and Hoover for a vacuum cleaner. Names like Portakabin, Sellotape, Shredded Wheat, Kleenex, Band-Aid, and many thousands more are registered brands. When you use these names you are referring to specific products. It is not necessary to specify that a brand is registered with a symbol, merely capitalise the first letter, and only the first letter, to indicate it is not generic. The UK Intellectual Property Office website, www.ipo.gov.uk carries a list to help but be warned that it is not complete

turgid is swollen and distended or in the case of language, pompous or bombastic not to be confused with **torpid** which means inactive or lethargic

try to, but never "try and"

Ulster is not Northern Ireland. Ulster is one of the four provinces of Ireland (the others are Munster, Leinster and Connaught) and includes six of the nine counties in Northern Ireland, which is part of the United Kingdom. Counties Donegal, Cavan and Monaghan are part of Ulster but in the Irish Republic

who or **whom** and when to use whom is a mystery to most people. Whom has almost disappeared from spoken English and sounds pompous so help it on its way and do not use it unless you know for sure when to use it in which case we need not explain the rule

viable does not mean feasible or practicable. It means capable of independent life. A foetus is viable but a plan is feasible

vocalised is a ridiculous was of saying said

Xerox, a trademark for the equipment that makes photocopies

yesterday, today, and other expressions of time ideally come at the start of a sentence but not at the expense of the most important element of the story. "Gordon Brown today called on the cabinet to resign."

Z is a fine letter with a great Scrabble score but if writing British English stick to S in word endings apart from the exceptions like capsize

Revision exercise

This is an opportunity to practice writing and apply the techniques described in this and the previous two chapters. The emphasis in this assignment is not on research and news gathering but about use of language and writing style.

Task 1

You have conducted an interview with Dr Margaret Heathstone, a leading campaigner against nuclear power. On the next page is a transcript of your interview with her. She has returned to the US and is on holiday so you cannot put any further questions to her. Write a 250-word story about what is wrong with nuclear power. For this task assume the story will be published as part of a larger feature about nuclear energy in a supplement in a national newspaper. Pay particular attention to choosing quotes that work and add to your piece.

Transcript of your tape

In response to your question, "what is wrong with nuclear power?" this is what Heathstone said:

No, the thing is in terms of its achievable potential, the financial and the social costs, and even carbon dioxide emissions, nuclear power is not an optimal solution. Everywhere one looks today, nuclear power seems to be resurging being portrayed as a safe and carbon-friendly source of electricity by its advocates.

This is Jacques Foos writing in a Scitizen column, writing [she quotes the headline] "No More Nuclear Energy? A Lost Fight Before It Even Starts!" Like this stuff from Daniel Gross in Newsweek [she quotes from the magazine] "nuclear power plants are the obvious fix for global warming and U.S. oil dependence."

Other papers are pushing the same line, here's the Economist. Look it proclaimed, when, let me see, in 2005, yes here, that nuclear power plants are the shape of things to come. They say that the Nuclear Regulatory Commission here in the US has received notice of application for 28 new nuclear units.

You know, contrary to such optimism, nuclear power plants will not be able to reduce greenhouse gas emissions in any meaningful timeframe.

Why? Well their financial costs are severe and there's the environmental and political costs as well that you have to consider. They are far from being a carbon neutral energy source.

OK, first, and this is in both the US and UK, if governments approved new nuclear units today, the earliest they would come online is 2015 - and that's presuming everything would go as planned.

Frank Barnaby and Kemp, James Kemp, they estimate that by 2075, and this is assuming that countries meet projections and would produce one-third of their electricity from nuclear sources, China would require around 530 Gigawatts India 600GW, the US 146GW, and Indonesia 125GW.

Taking an average reactor size of 1,000MW, this means 2,000 to 2,500 new nuclear reactors will be needed between now and then, you know that's around three a month. I mean this is completely unfeasible. You know even if the social and political, and the environmental concerns that I mentioned earlier could be wished away. Take France, that country currently generates 76 percent of its electricity from nuclear units. It has the fastest record for deploying nuclear plants in history, 58 between 1977 and 1993. What are we talking about here, an average of 3.4 reactors per year, not a month. I rest my case.

Even if just 700 new nuclear plants were constructed they would require the additional construction of 11 to 22 large enrichment plants. And that's not all, you're going to need 18 fuel fabrication plants. And waste disposal, consider that too, 10 waste disposal sites the size of Yucca Mountain. It's not a case that it may not be just undesirable, I wonder if it's technically impossible.

ENDS

Task 2

You have a commission from Publishing Today magazine to write a 150-word story about standards of local newspaper journalism. Publishers and editors of local newspapers and business magazines read Publishing Today so it is an ideal platform to show your talent to a wide audience.

The brief from the editor asks you to include the views of readers of the local paper and establish "what's the word on the street about the paper?" The editor suggests you take a specific local event to examine your local newspaper's reporting.

Write the 150 word story and for the purposes of this task make up quotes as needed. Although this is also a news writing exercise, concentrate on use of language, spelling and grammar.

Tips for Task 2

- *Start the sentence with a capital letter and end with a full stop.*
- *Use commas sparingly, no more than two in a sentence*
- *Use colons only to introduce quoted speech or a list*
- *Do NOT use semi colons or exclamation marks*
- *Use a question mark only in a quoted question never your text*
- *If in doubt about using an apostrophe leave it out*
- *Keep your sentences short*
- *Start the sentence with what is important then follow with the action, the verb*
- *Do not use verbs that end in ing - such as walking, shooting, crying. Use the active: walked, shot, cried.*
- *Forget descriptive words, the adjectives, such as boldly, carefully, happily. When used badly, which is more often than not, they turn good copy into flowery prose.*
- *Keep one idea per sentence*
- *Consider joining sentences if this improves flow when you revise the finished copy.*

Further reading

On writing:

William Strunk Jr and E B White, *The Elements of Style*, Longman (New York 1999)

John Seely, *Oxford A-Z of Grammar and Punctuation,* Oxford University Press (Oxford 2009)

Rudolph Flesch, *The Art of Clear Thinking* (1951),

Rudolph Flesch, *Lite English* (1983),

Grammar textbooks:

Michael Swan and Catherine Walter, *The Good Grammar Book*, Oxford University Press (Oxford 2001)

Michael Swan and Catherine Walter, *How English Works,* Oxford University Press (Oxford 1997)

John Eastwood, *Oxford Practice Grammar*, Oxford University Press (Oxford 1992)

HOW TO INTERVIEW

Interviewing is one of the key skills of a journalist, whether on the radio (such as John Humphreys on Radio 4's Today programme or Jeremy Paxman on TV's Newsnight) or for a newspaper or magazine article. A good interview, whether for an article on climate change for the *Guardian* or a new product for the trade publication *Plastics and Rubber Weekly*, provides the reader with words out of people's mouths, from an expert's opinion to a celebrity's anecdote or confession.

It sounds obvious, but reporters have to talk to people to learn what is really going on. More than that, however, journalists need to include people's voices in their stories to make those stories come alive. Interviewing takes preparation and skill. It is not just a matter of going out with a question and coming back with a sound bite.

Why interview?

A good interview elicits solid information from people and enables the journalist to obtain facts, opinions, and anecdotes for their news and features. The quotes add life to a piece and make it real. Newspapers and magazines want more than factual accounts of what happened. If there is a massive fire in a block of flats that kills three children it is no good simply telling the reader what took place, where and when. The journalist will interview witnesses, bystanders, neighbours, the police, and members of the family to build a more human-centred story. It is the quotes that make the piece unique.

The key

Interviewing is not as easy as it sounds because getting people to answer questions fully in interviews can be tricky. The key is to always ask open questions that begin with Who, What, Why, Where, When and How, outlined in the news chapter. These invariably get longer, more interesting answers.

What not to ask

There are four types of you should NOT ask:
1. Closed questions with only a 'yes' or 'no' answer (but if you forget, then immediately follow the yes or no answer with why?)
2. Questions that are too complicated to understand
3. Questions that contain incorrect facts
4. Questions that are too personal

Exercise One

1 Quickly, off the top of your head, think of three unusual questions to ask J K Rowling, author of the Harry Potter books.
2 Write them down.
3 Are they all open-ended?
4 If not, re-write the same questions so they start with one of the What, why, when, where, who and how words.

The importance of quotations

At the time of writing the pop star Michael Jackson had recently died. Without quotes from his family, former nannies and friends and pop stars the articles would have been dry and observational.

Are we dealing with a homicide or are we dealing with an accidental overdose... "I don't have that information," said police chief William Bratton, who told CNN that they are still waiting toxicology test results.

"I believe Michael was murdered, I felt that from the start. Not just one person was involved, rather it was a conspiracy of people." said La Toya Jackson.

Exercise Two

You are writing a feature for your local newspaper in the port town of Dover. The article is about P&O axing 300 jobs and the effect on the town.

1) Think of all the people who could be affected. Write a list.
2) Consider each person and imagine the problems the redundancies might cause them.

Types of interview

Face-to-face
The advantages of a face-to-face interview are that you can build up a rapport with the interviewee and that you generally have more time to explore issues. On the other hand, you might have to spend a day getting to the interview venue and back - you haven't written a word of the article at the end of it, and still face transcribing a tape the next day!

Whenever possible, conduct interviews face to-face says Chas J Hartman from *Scooping the News*, (www.scoopingthenews.com). He says that too many journalists resort to e-mail and telephone interviews in story situations where deadlines and locations do permit face-to-face interviews. Face-to-face interviews provide a sense of immediacy, the ability to ask quick follow-up questions, and the chance to really observe a source's response instead of just recording it.

Telephone
Probably the next best thing to a face-to-face interview is the telephone interview but you cannot weigh up gestures or body language to assess the interviewee. However, you can use your voice to persuade the interviewee and put them at ease.

In Sally Adams' book *Interviewing for Journalists*, she refers to a comment made by American writer John Brady. He said that telephone interviewing was the "MacDonald's of journalism - not the best method of getting information... but fast and serviceable."

The advantages of conducting an interview by telephone are that it saves time and money. A face-to-face interview   even for an hour - invariably takes a day once travelling is taken into account. Another advantage is that the interviewee might be a little more unguarded as they cannot see you writing, something that could be off-putting.

Another disadvantage is that the background can be too noisy and so impede the interview. Sally Nash once interviewed former Tory minister Steven Norris to the background of screaming when she was working from her mother's house and her neighbour had popped round with a toddler. When you are a freelancer working from home then washing machines and postmen ringing doorbells can be a nuisance and disturb the interview.

On a practical note try to keep your list of written questions separate from your answers when you are interviewing on the phone: do not just leave a gap underneath the question as you will probably find that you will run out of space.

When someone is speaking full throttle and you are trying to record as much as you can in longhand you might regret not learning Pittman's or Teeline. Shorthand is an exceptionally useful skill for a journalist but you need to use it daily to maintain your speed and accuracy.

E-mail

Journalists regularly use e-mail interviews because they are fast with have the advantage of providing the interviewee's words in black and white so you do not have to rely on your notes. Also, an email interview is particularly useful if someone is abroad and in a different time zone. There is still some resistance to the e-mail interview mainly because written answers lack the sparkle of quoted speech.

Step-by-step e-mail interviewing tips

• Introduce yourself and your news organisation, its circulation, and its importance to your community or readership.

• Explain just enough about your story or project to entice the source to participate.

• Make clear how you came across the source's name (someone referred you, etc.).

• Explain how you think their comments can add perspective or insight to your story.

• Provide your telephone number, geographic location, and other relevant contact information.

• Stress that you are on deadline. (Be clear about when you need responses by in order to meet your deadline.)

• Keep questions short, clear, and to the point with just one concept or inquiry per question.

• Let the source know that you will send a link or clip of the article when it is available. Then, set up a reminder so you deliver what you promised!

Preparation

Research is important before the interview in order to prepare the questions. The worst journalist is an uninformed journalist. Never, ever, enter into an interview without at least some level of prior knowledge about the topic or subject under discussion. At the first sign that a journalist is uninformed, many sources will immediately lose some level of respect for the reporter. You might need to establish background to a company or individual; you might need to find out what has already been written on the subject so you are not simply repeating what others have said. You might need to get to grips with a technical subject by reading articles.

Unless your shorthand is very good, using a voice-recorder is a good idea. Recording the interview means you can concentrate more on the conversation than on note taking, the quotations will be accurate, and you have a record of what the interviewee said if there are problems later. But never rely solely on recorders: like all technology they are prone to fail, usually at a critical moment. Recorders work well in controlled, indoor environments such as offices but even the latest digital recorders, which are a huge advance on tape recorders, struggle with back ground noises when used outdoors or in conference venues.

It does no harm to ask a few questions early on to which you know some of the answers. You will feel more in control of the interview and able to guide it in the direction you want it to go.

Joan Clayton, in her book *Interviewing for Journalists* (see Further Reading), believes that there are five main preparation stages before you actually meet your interviewee - Research, Arrange Appointment, Compile List of Questions, Check Equipment and Rehearse.

Although you can learn interviewing techniques from a course like this, it is only by doing real interview that you can practice and improve your technique.

Exercise Three

You have been commissioned to write an article on the future of retail supermarkets for Supermarketing Today.

According to your brief (a guide to what the commissioning editor wants you to cover in the piece) you should include the full range of supermarkets - from discount to upmarket. What can the customer expect to see in a year's time and in a decade's time?
1) Who will you interview?
2) What background research do you need to do?
3) Think of five good questions to ask

During the Interview

Never be afraid to ask for further information, to ask the interviewee to clarify a point or explain it more clearly. Nobody will mind if you say: "I'm sorry, do you mean?" It is better to get it straight at the time rather than have to call back once you have gone through your notes/tape etc and discovered that you do not understand what they have said!

One reason you are conducting this interview is to explain it to your readers. If your subject uses scientific jargon or explanations that only his or her peers would understand, politely interrupt and ask for further explanation. Never be embarrassed about not knowing something.

Take control of the interview. Never let the interviewee take charge, nor the press officer if they happen to be sitting in. Remember that you have a limited amount of time and that you need to get the information you came for. Do not be afraid to interrupt (politely) and move the conversation on if the interviewee is digressing or spending too long on one topic. Try to be interested (even if it is a façade!) in what the interviewee is telling you. You will get more out of them if they feel you are keen to hear what they have to say.

Silence is golden so let the interviewee fill it. Eventually you will have to ask the tough questions that your subject may be loath to discuss. When you start asking those provocative questions, the answers will most likely be short, or carefully worded. You may not get an answer at all. If this occurs, look your source in the eye and do not say a word. In most cases, the interviewee will begin to feel uncomfortable and begin to share information again.

Try to maintain eye contact. A reporter who spends most of the interview bent over taking notes or looking into a notebook can be as disconcerting as a tape recorder in an interviewee's face. Try to take abbreviated notes looking down only occasionally so you can focus on your interviewee. This will make the interview more like a conversation, and enable everyone to be more relaxed.

Never simply stick to a script in an interview. The best interviews are ones where fresh news comes to light because the reporter asked a good question, the source offered a revealing answer, or the journalist realised one of the source's answers warranted a follow-up question. It is good to prepare a basic set of key questions you want to cover in an interview, but always watch for opportunities to further explore answers given by a source.

Before you leave... ask your source if there is anything that you might have forgotten to ask.

After the interview

Review your notes straight after the interview while it is fresh in your mind. Now is the time to make your notes and comments in your notebook about what angles or what to check. Do not wait until the end of the day or later in the week to review your notes.

Off the record comments

This is the source of much confusion. Does it mean that the comment will not be reported? Or does that it will be reported but not attributed? It is important to establish the ground rules of the interview at the beginning. Be clear, produce your notebook and say: "This interview is on the record." When the interviewee says they are going off the record establish exactly what they mean: not to be reported at all or not to be attributed to them?

It is vitally important to get the interviewee back on the record and as soon as possible. Ask them: "Are we on the record now?" It is easy to spend an hour with someone who is off record so often that you have nothing for your story.

When can you use 'off the record' quotes?

The expression "off the record" is not in itself legally binding but that does not mean you can ignore the request. The *Scotsman*'s decision to publish comments made by Samantha Power, a senior aide to Barack Obama, in which she said: "[Hillary Clinton] is a monster too, that is off the record." prompted her resignation and a debate about the different standards of journalism in the US and UK. Gerri Peev, the *Scotsman*'s political correspondent, writing about the incident said:

> Say you are halfway through a taped interview and your subject is frank about a presidential candidate, then attempts to withdraw the remark, what should you do? Unless a deal has been struck in advance that the interview is off the record, I believe any journalist worth their ink should run the story.
>
> This happened to me when Power, then an adviser to Obama, delivered a candid assessment of Hillary Clinton during an interview to promote her book. She then tried to withdraw one of her quotes mid-flow, although no such agreement had been struck." I've found myself monstered in the American websites for this, but I cannot agree with Tucker Carlson, an MSNBC anchorman, who told me on air that "journalistic standards are so much dramatically lower in Great Britain than they are here [in the United States].

Korieh Duodu, in-house lawyer for the *Guardian* writing in the *Guardian's Media Section* said:

> The expression "off the record" is not in itself legally binding. But the circumstances of a conversation could conceivably give rise to obligations of confidentiality which might be upheld by the courts. An extreme example was an actor, Sally Farmiloe, who confided personal secrets to a journalist she considered a friend. The discussion was clearly off the record but the nature of the information was such that she was able to successfully sue for breach of confidentiality and privacy when those secrets were published in a newspaper.
>
> However, in the general run of cases, someone speaking off the record can rely on no more than a moral or ethical obligation on the journalist's part. And even if a legal obligation arises, that can be overriden if the information disclosed is sufficiently in the public interest to warrant publication.

Interviewing at press conferences

If you think it is going to be an interesting press conference, try to get to the front. You stand a chance of overhearing off-microphone interchanges. You may even get to buttonhole someone for a quick and exclusive interview. Do not forget that if you ask an interesting question and get an equally interesting response then everyone else at the press conference will benefit from it. If you have a chance to interview someone before or after the conference then keep your question to yourself. A good strategy is to follow up with a telephone call or an e-mail.

Top 10 interviewing tips

1 Do your homework. Find out about the company, product, and interviewee in advance

2 But do not trust Wilkepedia for background information

3 Write a list of questions that you think your readers would like the answered but do not feel you have to stick to them rigidly, they are a guide. Flexibility is paramount

4 Be on the lookout for a piece of information, an interesting snippet etc that will make your article stand out from the rest (and pick up on it and delve further instead of ploughing through your pre-set list of questions)

5 If face-to-face, make the most of your time to build up a rapport with your interviewee

6 Make sure that any quotations are accurate. Attribute the right quotation to the right person. Get the person's name (correct spelling) and title - pick up a business card if you are conducting the interview face-to-face

7 If travelling to an interview, plan your trip in advance so that you get there on time. Take a mobile phone in case of breakdowns, public transport problems etc

8 Be aware of what your clothes say about you. If interviewing a chief executive a suit or smart clothes may be in order but if you are interviewing a teenager, then more casual clothes might be suitable. If you are a woman, beware of being scantily clad - male interviewees may not be able to concentrate on the subject due to the distraction and, more rarely, some may offended

9 Press officers can be a help or a hindrance but use them wisely. They can be helpful in getting an interview set up in the first place and then checking facts for you and getting additional information

10 End the interview on a positive note. Thank the interviewee for their time; ask politely if you can call them again if you have any queries

Exercise Four

Interview an older member of your family - a parent/grandparent/aunt/uncle, etc, or an elderly next-door-neighbour, about either the so-called swinging 60s or food rationing in the war (depending on their age)

Make a provisional list of questions but do not be afraid to deviate from your questions if they go off on an interesting tangent.

Think how you could make the questions more original. Check if you are asking open or closed questions. Do you need to do any research?

After the interview, review the information you obtained. Could you have asked anything different to make the piece more interesting?

Exercise Five

This time you are going to interview the owner of your local shop or the landlord of a local pub. The theme of the article is how small shops and pubs have fared during the recession/over the last 12 months.

Prepare your questions and sound out your interview subjects. The interview should only last around 15-30 minutes. Think about:
- *When are you going to carry out the interview?*
- *Where will it take place?*

You can tell them that you are training to be a journalist and that you have a project to complete.

Review your notes and write up a short piece – around 350 words. Try to get some interesting, direct quotations into the article.

Exercise Six

You have been asked to write an article for a local Exeter newspaper, based on the press release shown below.

1) Read the release and make notes of possible questions/follow-ups

2) Make a list of possible interviewees. Think widely, both at local and national level - eg how does Exeter compare with other Devon councils? And nationally?

3) Use the telephone to call two of your interviewees. Say that you are writing an article as a training exercise

4) Write a short article – up to 400 words – based on your interviews

Press Release: Green scheme cuts council waste
New recycling schemes introduced in a Devon council's offices have helped reduce waste levels by 40%.

To help encourage recycling, six months ago staff at Exeter City Council were given greater access to recycling bins and individual waste bins were removed.

The result has delighted the council, which estimates that waste levels at the Civic Centre have been cut by 40%.

The schemes have also resulted in double the amount of paper, cardboard, plastic and cans being recycled.

Green awareness campaigns at the council have also led to an 80% drop in the number of computers being left on overnight, an 8% reduction in energy consumption and a 4% fall in the amount of paper being used.

Councillor Kevin Mitchell, Lead Councillor for Environment and Leisure, said: "We are absolutely delighted with the results of the awareness campaigns and the impact of the new recycling schemes.

"At the Civic Centre alone, this will mean a reduction of 260 large (1,100 litre) wheelie bins of waste being sent to landfill each year and that is down to the determined efforts of all staff."

The Environmental Champions scheme forms an integral part of the Council's Carbon Management Plan, which aims to reduce carbon dioxide emissions within the council by 20% by 2013.

Ends

Legalities of taping and notebooks

Most of the time, a notepad and pen are enough to record the interview. A reporter's notebook is the only evidence that courts will accept – tapes are worthless. Sometimes, if the subject is technical, scientific, complicated or could be tricky from a legal perspective, it might be useful to tape the interview. Digital recorders are best and come with software for Mac and PCs to load files and play back at different speeds, which helps when typing up interview notes. You can buy a small device that allows digital recorders to plug into your phone. But be wary of the laws surrounding privacy. Many question the ethics of recording phone calls without telling the other party so always advise people when you are taping calls and obtain their prior consent. There is a major drawback to recording interviews: the time necessary to playback and listen to the interview, and then to type the notes. It helps to be very disciplined in your questions if you use a recorded interview as the basis for an article.

Notebook discipline

It is important for a reporter to keep a tidy notebook and keep it handy too. When someone queries the facts of your story, it does not look good if you cannot find your notebook, let alone read what is in it. You may, admittedly on rare occasions, have to produce your notebook in court. Your credibility as a journalist is destroyed if you produce an unreadable mess of notes.

Always follow these notebook rules:

- Use a spiral bound notebook: it helps prove that you did not insert pages into the book after the writ landed on the editor's desk
- Date the cover with the date you started using the book and the date you finished it
- Rule off your notes at the end of each working day. Make sure you date the next section and every section
- Use catchlines for each story. If the notes and quotes for each interview are identified it is easier to spot the relevant notes in your book when you come to write up
- Put the date and time of the interview and the interviewee's name next to the catchline
- Never add notes to your book later on. Such cover-ups are easily exposed in court
- Keep your notebooks for at least two years. Libel actions have to start within 12 months of an article being published
- Put your name, address and telephone number on the inside cover of your notebook. You never know, someone may return it if you lose it
- Cross out with a thin line through the text. Do not obliterate and make unreadable any notes
- Be very clear to distinguish your notes or observations from any quotes or reported speech
- Write clearly. Your notebook is useless in court if no one else can read it. This is especially true of shorthand.

In practice, many journalists are extremely sloppy, forgetting to date their notebooks or their stories and use two or more books at the same time. If they had to present their books in court they would be littered with shopping lists, doodles or tips on which horse is likely to win the

3.40 at Derby! This is a dangerous practice. Your note keeping may not be perfect but at the very minimum keep your notebooks dated, work thorough each notebook systematically, date each interview or story notes and do not tear out pages

Before the interview

To get the best out of an interview you need to have a purpose or your questions will lack structure. Try to sell the article before you write it - this is particularly true if you are planning a face-to-face interview rather than a quick telephone or email interview. If you are a beginner, this might not be possible and you might have to send it to the publication 'on spec'. Editors who do not know you or your writing ability will want to read the piece before committing to publish it.

Try to settle on an angle for the piece and have some structured questions written before the interview. One journalist we know planned his questions in a logical, structured way so that he could simply write the article from the interviewees answers, in order. However, if the interviewee says something interesting outside your questions do not be afraid to change tack. You need judgement to weigh up what will make the most interesting angle.

How to conduct an interview

Tara Brabazon, professor of media studies at the University of Brighton, has seven rules of interviewing that journalists should note:
- Do not conduct an interview without preparation
- Second rule of interviewing: never conduct the session in a coffee shop
- Third rule of interviewing: do not rely on second-hand quotations and composite stories when material written by the subject is available
- Fourth rule of interviewing: beware journalists who interview you for more than 30 minutes. They have prewritten a story and are waiting for a headline
- Fifth rule of interviewing: read more than the introduction if you are going to talk in depth about a writer's work
- Sixth rule of interviewing: a shout-out on Twitter is not adequate preparation for an interview

• Seventh rule of interviewing: sort out any copyright and intellectual property rights issues on visual content before switching on the camera

Exercise Seven

Listen to an interview on a good TV or radio programme - BBC's Today programme or Channel 4 News are suggestions - and note:

1) Does the interviewer use open or closed questions?
2) How does the interviewer take charge of the interview? Things to note here are interrupting if the interviewee goes on at length, repeating questions (Jeremy Paxman-style).
3) Does the interviewer follow a line of questioning or is the interview more unstructured?
4) How does the interviewer bring the interview to an end?

Radio and TV interviewing techniques are different in that the interview itself is presented to the listener or viewer. For print work, you filter the results when you write the report but the questioning is the same. The John Humphreys and Jeremy Paxman style of interview, at times is very aggressive. It works for them because they have formidable reputations built over many years. They are not role models for novice reporters.

Revision exercise
Here is this chapter's revision exercise

The Task
1) Interview a friend by telephone, e-mail or face-to-face about his/her views on the recession for a piece for the Guardian about personal experiences on surviving the credit crunch. We have provided an example story below. Structure your questions beforehand. Write your notes in a reporter's notebook. Now write up the piece with plenty of quotes. Find an angle. Do not exceed 250 words.

This is an example story

Things have got better and worse in the micro-economy that retired civil servant Margaret Spink manages in her house on the Servia estate in central Leeds. Her summer backup of fresh vegetables from her garden has been decimated by slugs and Cabbage White caterpillars; but the gradual recovery of shares has seen her savings slightly increase.

At 76, ill-health is a constant bother and, like the garden pests, it has also sabotaged her financial plan for the second half of the year. She had banked on turning off the central heating, but a persistent condition has forced her to leave it on. "I get cold very quickly now, even on warm days outside," she says. "That's why that radiator's hot, even though I'm sitting here wearing my overcoat."

The marginally higher dividend cheques in Spink's bank account are the result of prudent saving during her long career in Leeds, where she worked her way up the civil service grades after coming to the city from Teesside, originally to work as a nanny. But her modest portfolio, which supplements her combined OAP and civil service pension of £482 a week, has not seen any spectacular bull runs; most of the holdings are small and in institutions such as Lloyd's bank, which still has enormous problems of its own.

Her outgoings, meanwhile, increase slowly. Monthly rent for the house to Leeds city council has gone up £4 from £300 and her latest monthly power bill was £108, compared to £100 in February. Her eight grandchildren and four great-grandchildren still get their £15 birthday money - one expense she is determined to keep up. One of them qualified for her £30 bonus at age 18 this year. "Two more are due for that next year," she says. "But it's the young that need a hand. I can keep up my own spirits. You have to."

Her 11-year-old Labrador Kimber has also made one of those unexpected holes that hit the most prudent budgets; diabetes has made the dog nearly blind and means regular, large bills at the vet's. There's not been time, either, to get the £14,000 caravan at Skegness, which she bought as an investment, into a fit condition for letting. "But the family has had lots of use of it," she says. "So in that way, it's been earning its keep while this recession goes on."
Ends 400 words

Further reading

Sally Adams, Wynford Hicks, *Interviewing for Journalists*, Routledge, 2009
Joan Clayton, Judy Piatkus, *Interviewing for Journalists*, 1994
Ann Dix, Heinemann, *Teeline Fast*, 1990
Dawn Johnston, *Teeline for Journalists*, Heinemann, 2006

HOW TO WRITE FEATURES

A feature editor summed up what it takes to make a good feature saying: "You have to make it sing and dance, not drag its feet." It is a good lesson: it takes practice and skill to achieve that. Let us start by considering what a feature story is. First things first: a feature is not a long news story. Features can be defined negatively as all the editorial matter in a newspaper, magazine or radio or TV schedules which is factual but not news (in the sense of happened immediately). Feature articles are non-fiction articles that intend to inform, teach, or amuse the reader on a topic. A feature article is an umbrella term that includes many literary structures such as personality sketches, essays, how-tos, interviews, and many others.

It follows that products such as monthly magazines must consist almost entirely of feature material. Newspapers, which cannot break news stories as fast as the electronic media, have a mixture of news and features. The same is true of scheduled/formatted news shows on radio and TV, such as *The Today Programme, Newsnight, Channel Four News*, that mix genuine news with mini-features to fill the scheduled programme length.

It is often said of newspapers (and electronic news programmes) "people come for the news, but stay for the features." Features are also very important in setting the "tone" for newspapers. Features are not defined by newness or exclusivity. They can deal with what is simply interesting, remarkable, or entertaining. However, it is essential that features be planned. Structure is vital. The danger is that features often ramble or digress and then peter out with no real ending which is frustrating for the reader. Unlike news stories, the feature must have a proper ending, a climax, or a pay-off.

The feature form allows for more self expression and personal style by the writer because it is less formulaic than the traditional news story, but with that comes pitfalls. When you are beginning you will not go far wrong if you adopt the same workmanlike approach as news and keep to the active voice and short sentences, as described in the news writing chapter.

Ensure that your feature has changes of pace, lack of waffle, keeps to the point, and has a narrative drive from beginning to end.

Some differences between news and features...

News	Features and documentaries
Telling	Seeing (inc "word pictures" on radio)
Brief/Summary	Lengthy/ detailed
Aimed at whole audience	Aimed at "niche" sections of the readership
Length varies (importance)	Length fixed by editorial structure/
Defined styles	Many styles/ generic types
Pictures useful	Pictures essential/ graphics
Published instantly	Published according to schedule
Event-led ("news agenda")	Production-led (fitting the magazine

Exercise One
Look through three different print publications and identify a feature from each.

Write down its:

1) length

2) type of style

3) number of quotations

4) does the introduction reel you in?

5) is the feature interesting enough to make you want to continue reading?

5) does it just end in mid-air or is the ending satisfying?

Introductions

When starting to write a feature, you need to grab the readers' attention, to make them want to stop whatever they are doing and want to read. Finding that "hook" is one of the hardest aspects of feature writing. Before you even start typing, think about how you are going to achieve your goal of communicating to your audience in a way that - to cite the guiding principles of the BBC - educates, informs, and entertains. How do you do this? There are a number of techniques you can use, from using a quotation to using an interesting statistic. The first paragraph outlines the subject or theme of the article. It may also:

- provoke the reader's interest by making an unusual statement
- provide any necessary background information.
- invite the reader to take sides by making a controversial statement
- heighten the drama of an event or incident to intensify its appeal
- establish the writer's tone
- create a relationship between the writer and the reader.

Consider these three real introductions to features show below. Even a dry "unsexy" subject can be made interesting if the writer is skilful enough.

From *Marie Claire*: My big fat crush

> In 1989, I was an obese 17-year-old virgin whose one solace was scribbling my deepest desires and darkest thoughts into my diary. 'Back then, I genuinely believed there was no chance I would ever lose my virginity. I was a 14-and-a-half-stone fat girl stuck in a small Lincolnshire market town: a big girl in a sea of thin girls, with an aching desire for a man. Unfortunately, this desire could only be satisfied with the sweet cuddle of a four-finger Kit-Kat. Or two, or three. Or, on a really bad day, five. Food was my lover, as the graveyard of Twix wrappers hidden behind my bed would testify.

From the *New Scientist* by David Shiga: Why the universe may be teeming with aliens

> WANTED: Rocky planet outside of our solar system. Must not be too hot or too cold, but just the right temperature to support life.
>
> It sounds like a simple enough wish list, but finding a planet that fulfils all of these criteria has kept astronomers busy for decades.

Until recently, it meant finding a planet in the "Goldilocks zone" - orbiting its star at just the right distance to keep surface water liquid rather than being boiled off or frozen solid.

Now, though, it's becoming increasingly clear that the question of what makes a planet habitable is not as simple as finding it in just the right spot. Many other factors, including a planet's mass, atmosphere, composition and the way it orbits its nearest star, can all influence whether it can sustain liquid water, an essential ingredient for life as we know it. As astronomers explore newly discovered planets and...

And this from the *Financial Times* by Andrew Jack, pharmaceuticals correspondent: Flu's unexpected bonus

With over 96 countries stockpiling oseltamivir, Andrew Jack assesses who has benefited from pandemic flu

Former US defence secretary Donald Rumsfeld was talking about weapons of mass destruction and the war in Iraq when he referred to "unknown unknowns" in 2002, but he could just as easily have been explaining why drug companies have been able to make money out of the global flu pandemic. Within a few months of his comments, a series of events began to fuel growing international concern about a new pandemic. The mixture of fear and ignorance over its timing, nature, and severity soon sparked an unexpected bonanza for the manufacturers.

Since the emergence of swine flu in Mexico this spring finally triggered the first pandemic in four decades, J P Morgan, the investment bank, estimates that governments have made fresh orders for antiviral drugs of $3bn (£1.8bn; 2bn) and that recent or potential sales of vaccines are $7bn.1 All that despite signs that the virus is proving relatively mild....

Exercise Two

Consider the three stories above.

1) Which introduction appeals to you most? Give a reason.

2) Identify and list some of the techniques the writers used to make their introductions compelling?

3) Look at the headlines - do the headlines make you want to read on? Why?

Headlines and Standfirsts

It most cases the publication or web site provide the headline and standfirst, the short introduction to the feature. However, a good attention-grabbing headline and standfirst are equally as important when supplying copy 'on spec' to an editor as part of a pitch and your article is more likely to be read and considered for publication.

Feature formats

The key to feature writing is to understand the various formats such as the news feature; the consumer review; confessional interview; profiles and investigations and so on.

A newspaper will tend to have a profile on page X; a comment piece on page Y; a news feature over the first few pages after the proper news pages; a horoscope on page Z; a feature interview with a sports star on the cover of the sports supplement and so on. Magazines are even more heavily formatted (advertising is sold to be included next to a particular type of feature). All of this is also true of the trade press; and specialist consumer magazines.

Ideas

Once you have a track record and a portfolio of published work editors will be more likely to approach you with a request for a feature. Initially though and even when you are established you will be submitting ideas for features.

It is a good idea to save relevant news stories as launching points and ready-made research for your articles. Gather publications that serve your target market, and look for ideas that relate to your business.

Study your chosen publications and determine the types of stories each of them seems to favour, then use them as starting points for your own ideas. Look for patterns, trends, and points of discussion.

Remember: few story ideas are truly original. A new slant, an interesting angle, timeliness, and focus; these are enough to make a story publishable.

Shown below is a real feature pitch to a specialist transport magazine editor. It is the sort if thing that you will have to do over and over again. You will be rejected but persevere. If one magazine does not like the idea, put a spin on it and try again somewhere else. Please note that in this example the tone is very familiar: the journalist in this case has a long-established working relationship with this particular editor. In this instance, the writer brainstormed ideas, using the Internet to source topical issues related to the keywords 'transport law'. She also took stories that appeared in the news section of this publication (and similar magazines) – in print and online – and suggested further research to develop them into features.

Here is the e-mail from the journalist and the editor's reply are shown below:

Hi Pat,

Here is the reminder e-mail you suggested last week about doing some stuff for CM's legal section!

I had a think and have come up with a few ideas although you may have some yourself of course and could have covered some of these anyway...

1) Data protection - a lot in the news about this so topical following the Joseph Rowntree Report which suggests that some government databases may be illegal (CM could look at which databases drivers are on and also what about the Driver CPC - who will have access to those records etc?)

2) ACAS code of practice on discipline and grievances has been agreed by Parliament. It is expected to make it easier for employers to resolve disputes at an early stage and should help reduce the number of employment tribunal claims.

3) Clamping - the government is trying to 'clamp down' on the clampers. We have had a lot of complaints about over-zealous clamping at T&D. The article would look at what are the rights of the driver/operator and what the new legislation could achieve.

4) Redundancies - legal onus on operator, what about employee. I'm sure you have already covered this (!) but certainly worth a look at if not...

5) Illegal immigrants stowing away on trucks seems to be becoming a hot issue again. Recently RoadTransport.com featured the case of a haulier who was fined £78,000 for stowing away illegal immigrants. What are the latest guidelines, what can hauliers and drivers do to protect themselves.

See what you think Pat!
Best wishes,
Sally

Pat's e-mail response:

Dear Sally
Give me a ring - I'm quite keen on clamping and immigrants but would like to talk to you first before sending briefs.
Patric

The eventual brief is shown below:
Dear Sally,
COMMERCIAL MOTOR LEGAL BRIEF
SUBJECT: NEW WHEEL CLAMPING REGS (3 PAGES)
AUTHOR: SALLY NASH
COPY DATE: 29 APRIL   ISSUE DATE: 7 MAY 2009
WORDS: 1300 (3 PAGES)   RATE: £325 PLUS EXPENSES

Please set out the proposed changes to regulations governing wheel clamping and how, in particular, they will affect our readers.

How Is wheel clamping governed now and what are the problems with the current rules?

We have run a number of features on this subject prompted by complaints from readers who have been charged £250 for just stopping to use a toilet. This is a greater fine than that for many quite serious road traffic offences - for example, £200 is the maximum penalty under the Graduated Fixed Penalty scheme.

Talk to the British Parking Association; trade associations, operators and the Home Office. Is £250 the kind of excessive penalty the government has in its sights?

If changes go ahead what are the timelines?

SIDEBAR
Bullet point the proposed changes and include any useful websites, contacts etc

Thanks, Pat

Feature structure

Paul Benedetti, a journalism instructor at the University of Western Ontario and a freelance writer identifies the "Big Lie" of writing as starting with a great lead and just writing until you are finished. Instead, he says, a good feature needs an outline and should hook the reader like a three-act play does, with a complication, some development, and a resolution. Sometimes the angle will reveal itself through the gathering and reviewing of information, but sometimes you will need to write to a particular brief, for example if you are commissioned. This will then dictate the angle you adopt - or whether you get paid!

The middle section of an article consists of a number of paragraphs that expand the main topic of the article into subtopics. The usual components are:

- subheadings
- facts and statistics that support the writer's opinion
- personal viewpoints
- opinions from authorities and experts
- quotes and interviews
- anecdotes and stories
- specific names, places and dates
- photographs, tables, diagrams, and graphs.

Exercise three

Choose one subject that you have a real interest in: this could be anything from ballroom dancing to scuba diving to stamp collecting!

1 Try to identify some outlets for a feature on your subject - do not forget the national newspapers which carry features pages, particularly at the weekend. Also, online websites might be enthusiastic about taking on a short feature. List three possible outlets.

2 Think of three features ideas on your subject. How will you persuade an editor to accept them?

3 Write a draft e-mail to the editor of one of the publications you have identified. Outline your ideas and why the editor should accept them, eg, are they topical? Can you get hold of someone key on the subject to interview? Do you have an interesting angle on the subject?

Endings

Unlike a news story, features are not written with an information pyramid. There is more art to the feature story so the end of the feature is as important as the introduction.

All sorts of devices can end a feature. Here are some suggestions:
• a comment
• arguing a case / drawing a conclusion
• a concluding quote
• a pointed question
• a summary of the article
• indeed, many of the devices used to start it - but it helps to:
• hold something significant back and
• make a connection with the introduction.

Good features are not easy to write. Beware of opting for a safe subject that has been done to death!

Exercise Four

Shown below is a news story posted on Channel 4's website. Try to come up with a pitch for a feature for the health section of women's magazine Bella. Will you move away from the scientific thrust?

1) What is your angle for the feature?

2) Who will you be talking to for quotes for the piece?

3) Use some of the facts in the news story and write the introduction to the feature. Remember that you are trying to engage the reader and draw them in so feel free to embellish/add to/change the details. However, you must also include some of the facts as illustrated in the Channel 4 news piece. Do not exceed 200 words for your intro. A good tip here is to focus on one child - make this up if necessary.

Bone marrow breakthrough eases treatment
by Jenny Wivell

Children needing bone marrow transplants could be spared chemotherapy side effects after doctors develop a new technique to prevent rejection.

A new life saving technique has been developed to treat terminally ill children in need of bone marrow transplants. Patients with Primary Immunodeficiencies (PID) can now be given antibodies instead of standard chemotherapy to prepare them for transplants.

The technique pioneered by doctors at Ormond Street Hospital and the UCL Institute of Child Health is more effective and has fewer side effects than traditional chemotherapy which can cause organ damage and infertility.

Dr Persis Amrolia, a consultant in bone marrow transplants at GOSH who led the research published today in The Lancet said: "Because this technique gives us an alternative to intensive chemotherapy, the treatment we can offer is safer, and provides a greater chance of allowing these children to grow up to lead normal healthy lives.

"We didn't see any of the hair loss and sickness normally associated with intensive chemotherapy for BMT, there was much less damage to the liver, lungs and gut and we anticipate none of the harmful long-term side effects.

"This represents a major breakthrough in how we treat patients who have PID."

The technique has been used to save the lives of 13 out of 16 children too sick to undergo a traditional bone marrow transplant, over the last ten years.

As well as being cured of their underlying diseases, they also recovered twice as quickly as those given the standard treatment. Fifty children with PID receive a transplant each year in the UK.

Dr Amrolia from GOSH added: "Because this approach was experimental, we only used it on the sickest children, who we felt could not tolerate standard transplant chemotherapy.

"Given how sick these children were before transplant, the results are remarkable. What's really encouraging is that pretty much all the children who survived now have a really good quality of life."

The significant improvement in outcome for PID patients has led to many European and US centre adopting this as standard care, but ultimately similar approaches could be used to treat children with other genetic diseases and even leukaemia.

ENDS

Exercise Five

Come up with five feature ideas that you think *Marie Claire* would be interested to publish. Try to make them global, topical and related to women's issues. You might need to do some background research to give you some initial stimulus – if you can, try to get hold of a recent copy and note the types of feature being commissioned.

Exercise Six

The following is an article published on *Community Care*'s website. Read it and note:

1) how the writer uses a tip box at the end – see the section on sidebars

2) how the writer provides a list of key points – some of these might slow down the article so it is often a good idea to take these out and put them in a separate list or box.

Good Practice: Norfolk-based charity Break, UEA and Frank Buttle Trust
Inspiring and supporting young people formerly in care to university education, by Camilla Pemberton

Charities such as Break in Norfolk, and many universities are pointing the way forward when it comes to helping care leavers enter higher education. Camilla Pemberton reports

Preparing for university does not happen overnight. The skills that equip students for university life are often learned through early experiences at home and in education. But for care leavers these experiences are likely to have been disrupted, which might go some way to explaining why only 6% of looked-after children go on to university.

In recent years, the government and a growing number of universities have taken steps to address this, and now provide more opportunities than ever for care leavers to enter higher education. Local authorities and universities are also working together to improve the educational outcomes of looked-after children.

The University of East-Anglia (UEA) is one of the latest universities to be awarded a quality mark by grant aid body the Frank Buttle Trust for excellence in meeting the needs of care leavers - one of 50 so far. The university provides bespoke taster days for local children's services and offers children the chance to attend summer schools with their foster carers and care workers. "We are introducing university to children early, so that they can aim high and work towards a goal," says Louise Bohn, UEA's outreach manager.

Twenty one-year-old Jarone Macklin-Page (pictured) was supported by Norfolk-based charity Break, to go into higher education. Now a student at London's Italia Conti Academy of Theatre Arts, he says care leavers with the potential to go to university must be encouraged through a culture of confidence-building and practical advice.

When Macklin-Page moved into a children's home he never thought he would go to university. But, during his five years at the home his ambition to succeed was developed through sporting activities, holidays and work opportunities organised by Break. He particularly enjoyed a film project, where £7,000 was raised so a group of young people could produce short films. "It taught me to value personal achievement," Macklin-Page says.

Break's care leavers are assigned a transition worker to ensure they are supported in planning their futures. Macklin-Page met regularly with transition worker Claire Tuthill. When he expressed an interest in performing arts, Tuthill arranged for him to speak with a drama graduate before helping him fill out his Ucas form. "I was encouraged to really think about what I wanted for my future," says Macklin-Page. Tuthill then liaised with his social worker, local authority and university representatives to make suitable arrangements.

As a result, Macklin-Page's educational and accommodation costs are covered by the government, and Break looks to cover any additional costs through fundraising. Some grants are paid in lump sums so Macklin-Page has been taught how to budget. He was also told what to expect.

"I'm lucky to have year-round accommodation, which some universities can't offer," he says. "But I was warned about friends disappearing home during the holidays."

Break staff continue to support care-leavers for as long as they need. Stephen Norman, of the National Care Advisory Service, says this is good practice: "The reassurance of continued contact and support gives young people the freedom to make educational choices," he says.

Chris Hoddy, divisional director of care for Break, adds: "We prepare our children to be self-motivated and productive, whether in employment or higher education. We encourage them to achieve their full potential and have the same aspirations for them as for our own children."

And Macklin-Page believes it is this ethos that made the possibility of attending university a reality. "It gave me the ambition to get to university, as well as the confidence to enjoy it."

Sidebar
The Frank Buttle Trust: http://www.buttletrust.org
Break http://www.break-charity.org
Key Points
• Care leavers in higher education are supported until they are 25.
• As of 2006, full-time UK students from low-income homes are entitled to a non-repayable government maintenance grant. Most care leavers will be entitled to the full amount of £2,906.
• The government provides all UK universities with an Access to Learning Fund to dispense each year. Bursaries from this fund are means tested and range from £100 to £3,000.
• Care leavers should check the box on their Ucas form to indicate their care leaver status.
• Check with The Frank Buttle Trust to see which universities carry a quality mark.

Sidebar
What works - Tips from care leaver and, now, graduate Clare Fearns:
When Clare Fearns, 26, applied to university after being in foster care she received little support. Despite this, she graduated from the University of York with a sociology degree, and is now studying for a masters in social work at the University of Durham. She advises any professional supporting a care leaver into higher education to:
• Make sure somebody helps the young person settle in on their first day.
• Research the local area with them and encourage them to join activities, like sports teams or community theatre groups, or to seek part-time work. This builds support networks if they can't return home or to their carers during the holidays.

• Make sure you find the time to regularly communicate with them to see how they are getting on, and remind them regularly how much they have achieved to get there.
ENDS

Exercise Seven
1) Read the press release below and write a list of at least three types of publications that might be interested in running a feature on the subject matter .
2) Come up with an angle for each publication.
3) What extra information would you need for each feature?
4) Who would you need to interview for the piece?
5) Write a snazzy introduction for one of your articles – make up any quotes and other information that you feel is necessary.

New straight-to-server digital recording technology will boost efficiency and cut costs for UK police
   Innovative solution from Indico Systems will revolutionise the way that police interviews are recorded, accessed and stored
Indico Systems, a world leader in secure digital recording solutions, has today unveiled its latest straight-to-server digital recording system, an innovative solution that has been optimised for use within the criminal justice sector. The new system, known as Indico Streaming Server, has already enjoyed great success in Scandinavia, and is now being implemented at Teesside University, Triangle Services, and offered on a trial basis to selected UK police forces.
   When connected to Indico Video (the room-based recording solution) Indico Streaming Server will allow police forces across the UK to stream their audio and/or video interviews onto a secure digital server platform, so that they can be accessed quickly by typists, or by detectives wanting to review and bookmark interviews, regardless of their location. Authorised personnel can even monitor the interview remotely - in real time - and for added time-savings, can also mark the recording with digital "bookmarks", thereby making it easier to find specific parts of an interview.

"At the moment, UK police forces typically record interviews on tapes or CDs or other removable media that then need to be sealed, labelled, sent to a typist, and then stored securely," says Simon Jones, Sales and Marketing Director, Indico Systems UK. "Unfortunately, because of the need to manage, store and sift through such a large amount of data, a serious strain is being put on police resources. Plus, there are inherent security risks involved with sending such important information via an internal postal system, not to mention delays. It can take up to several days for a tape to reach a typist, which can obviously delay court proceedings dramatically. Any subsequent copies can take much longer."

Although some police forces have already moved from analogue to digital technology for the recording of their investigative interviews, Indico Systems takes this model to the next level. In addition to making high-quality digital audio and video recordings that can be stored on digital discs using Indico Video, Indico Streaming Server store digital copies of every police interview on a secure network, which means that there is no risk of CD's or DVD's being lost, damaged or delayed in transit.

Until now, considerable delays have been caused by the time it takes for removable media to be delivered to transcribers who then summarise each interview. With Indico Server, however, the interview is recorded straight onto the server, which means that these delays and associated costs are eliminated.

In 2008, Lancashire Constabulary used similar technology to replace traditional taped interviews with digital recording methods as part of a Government-approved pilot study. Instead of using traditional tapes, interviews were stored on a secure server which legal teams and police were able to access.

"With analogue tape systems proving increasingly unreliable, a move to digital recording - and ultimately a server-based solution - is now widely accepted as the way forwards for UK police forces," continued Simon Jones, Indico Systems UK. "The Lancashire study concluded that up to three hours were saved per interview by using a server solution to record and store the interviews. If you multiply this figure by up to 40 interviews per day across a force, and then extrapolate those figures across the whole of the UK, you can quickly see how the police, the government, and the taxpayer can save hundreds of thousands of pounds with this approach. Not only that, but less police time wasted also means more time spent on front line crime fighting."

Indico Systems complies with the Police and Criminal Evidence Act 1984 (PACE), an Act of Parliament which provided a legislative framework for the powers of police officers in England and Wales, as well as codes of practice for the exercise of those powers. The Indico Video solution makes sure that current PACE requirements are met in terms of the number of copies created, and the system also makes and retains hard copies of every interview that is recorded.

Indico Video is extremely easy to use, as it features a robust touchscreen interface that supports all aspects of the interview management process: Indico Streaming Server has been specially designed to integrate into existing IT network environments with minimum disruption.
ENDS

About Indico Systems
Established in 2000 and with offices in Norway, Denmark, the UK and Estonia, Indico Systems develops, installs and maintains a range of secure digital recording solutions for a wide variety of applications, most notably within the police and criminal justice sectors, healthcare applications, defence and intelligence.

Indico Systems is committed to delivering class-leading software solutions for a variety of applications, as well as supporting an increasing network of European customers. Recent UK successes also include; The University of Portsmouth, Gloucestershire Constabulary, Teesside University and Triangle Services. Its solutions, services and support are delivered via a dedicated team of developers, technical account managers and sales professionals. For more information, please visit http://www.indicosys.com

Exercise Eight

1) *Read the news story below from the Guardian*
2) *Write an outline for a feature in the Times Education Supplement (TES), including what you will put in each of three sections (remember the 3 Act drama?)*
3) *Who will you interview?*

Chocolate, crisps and sugary drinks will be banned from secondary school canteens this month, under new rules to tackle childhood obesity.

The nutritional standards, already in force in primary schools, require a school lunch to contain at least one portion of vegetable or salad and a portion of fruit. School canteens will not be allowed to offer meals outside strict calorie limits, and must provide foods with a minimum level of iron, zinc, calcium and vitamins. Salt will be removed from canteen tables and foods that have too much fat, saturated fat and sugar will not be allowed.

Drinks will be limited to water, low-fat milk and juice. Schools have been told to use reduced-fat spreads rather than butter and to spread this thinly.

Meals that pass the new nutritional standards test include breaded fish, spicy fajitas, yoghurt and some cakes. The new rules follow a high-profile campaign by celebrity chef Jamie Oliver to improve the quality and taste of the country's school lunches.

The change comes as ministers were criticised for promising free lunches for all primary school children in two deprived parts of the country.

Until now, free school meal have been available only to children living in homes with an annual income of less than £16,040, which is about 15.9% of primary pupils, and 13.1% of secondary pupils.

But, from this month, all pupils in Newham, east London, and County Durham will receive free lunches as part of a £40m, two-year trial to improve behaviour, health and academic standards and change eating habits in their homes.

It would cost £1bn to provide free school meals to all children in primary schools in England.

The Soil Association, a charity that supports organic farming, said the government should concentrate on providing free lunches to all children below the poverty line, rather than all pupils in just two areas of the country.

Ministers should also ensure that school canteens are well-equipped, the charity said. Jeanette Orrey, a former dinner lady who now works for the Soil Association, said: "I'm all for free school meals, but my plea to the government is to first make sure schools have adequate dining facilities and overworked school catering staff have the hours and capacity within the kitchen to cope with free school meals to all. The quality of the food and the dining experience must not be jeopardised in a rush to universal free school meals."

A survey of local authorities by the Conservatives revealed that three in 10 schools do not have proper kitchens.

Opposition MPs said ministers could not afford to roll out free school meals for all children.

Ed Balls, the schools secretary, said: "Eating a nutritious meal at lunchtime from a young age can help improve the behaviour of children in school and at home - that's why these pilots are so important. Healthy school meals are vital to helping children do well at school and to prevent obesity. I encourage all families who are entitled to a free school meal to claim this valuable support."

He added: "We want to make sure that children are getting a healthy, balanced meal at school, which is why we have introduced the new nutrient standards. Teenagers are the hardest group to reach but that doesn't mean giving up. We must simply work harder to encourage them away from the takeaway and into their school canteen."

A survey by the School Food Trust last week found a fifth of low-income families in England were not checking to see if they could claim free school meals for their children, worth £700 a year.

Revision exercise
The following is a real commission from Good Housekeeping magazine.

Editor's Alert: Freelance Journalist Needed: Sent at: 24 Sep 2009
I'm looking for a freelance journalist to write an in-depth first-person piece. I am Good Housekeeping's Deputy Features Editor and am on the lookout for a feature - synopsis is below.

We would like an in-depth first-person piece with a woman, 35 upwards, with child or children, who took a financial knock because of the downturn (it could be redundancy, bankruptcy, demotion, whatever) but has come through it. The knock would need to have had tangible effects on her lifestyle - perhaps she had to downsize her home, move to a cheaper part of the country, generally scale down her material expectations and her lifestyle.

I also imagine it would have caused a strain within her relationship and made family life hard for a while. But the idea is that she has coped, come through with her family intact and has learned to like her new way of living. There will obviously have been tough times, but we would like her to have discovered something new in life as a result and be happy with her lot...

It would be a 1200-word first-person feature, the fee would be £750 and I would need the copy in the next three weeks or so. Please only email if you can help.
If you had any ideas, pls contact me - all my details are below.
Cheers,
Laura Mannering, Deputy Features Editor

What you need to do
1) Imagine that you have a friend that matches this description: she has lost her job in banking so she and her family (husband and two sons) have been forced to move out of London to Hertfordshire. The marriage has been under strain as a result of money worries, added to which there is the threat of her husband losing his job too. Add any further details as you see fit...alternatively devise an alternative 'scenario' and write this up. Do not forget that Laura is looking for a "triumph through adversity" type of feature.

2) Write the list of questions that you would ask your friend and make up the replies.

3) Write feature (500 words max), paying particular attention to the introduction, quotations (made up, the more dramatic the better in this sort of piece) and the ending. Good luck!

4) Write a practice e-mail to Laura Mannering, pitching your idea

Further reading

Linda Formichelli, *Renegade Writer: A Totally Unconventional Guide to Freelance Writing Success*, Marion Street Press (2005)

Edward Jay Friedlander, *Feature Writing for Newspapers and Magazines: The Pursuit of Excellence*, Allyn & Bacon (2000)

Brendan Hennessy, *Writing Feature Articles*, Focal Press (2005)

Brendan Hennessy, *Writing Feature Articles: A Practical Guide to Methods and Markets*, Focal Press (1996)

Peter Jacobi, *The Magazine Article: How to Think it, Plan it, Write it,* Indiana University Press (1997)

Linda Jones, *The Greatest Freelance Writing Tips in the World*, The Greatest in the World (2007)

Susan Pape, *Feature Writing: A Practical Introduction,* Sage Publications (2006)

Dawn B Sova, *How to Write Articles for Newspapers and Magazines* (Arco How to Write Articles for Newspapers & Magazines) Peterson's Guides (2002)

Sharon Wheeler, *Feature Writing for Journalists* (Media Skills), Routledge (2009)

HOW TO SUB-EDIT

Subbing or sub-editing is more than just a process for checking copy: it is how you present copy to suit the particular medium or publication. This chapter is the follow on to the earlier chapter on the Language of Journalism but here we learn the techniques for removing the mistakes and practice them with a series of exercises.

Whereas most people edit their writing, journalists sub their copy. There is an important difference. As a journalist, you are doing more than just checking that there are no spelling errors; you are crafting the material to suit a particular publication, outlet and audience.

Subediting is the most important skill you can acquire as a journalist because it is how you improve your copy. Even the most practiced professional writer will need to sub their copy. It is how you polish and perfect the words and sentences to take your writing from good to excellent.

Who are the sub editors?
Sub editing is a job on its own and newspapers employ large teams of sub-editors. Even small weekly newspapers carry a sub or two on the permanent staff. In the past few years, the number of sub-editors employed has diminished although the importance of the role has not reduced.

In most cases, the main function of staff on small magazines, whatever the job title, is sub-editing. The sub editor's role is increasingly defined in magazine production terms with page layout and make-up added to the tasks the sub performs.

The sub editor's role, like that of proofreaders who have long disappeared, is increasingly subsumed into other production jobs such as design and layout. Most editors' jobs on small magazines, web sites, and business-to-business magazines are little more than sub-editing roles.

Computers and their associated technology have radically changed the print industry and not always for the better. An early casualty was the traditional role of sub editor, whose loss is evident in the very poor standards of much published material. Computers have reduced the costs of print production and removed many of the skills needed. Unfortunately in a bid to save money, many publishers also removed the skills, like sub editing, necessary to maintain quality. The onus is now on the journalist to provide copy, and often at a lower rate of pay, that is perfect in every sense. Much of the work the sub editor did, now rests with you, the writer.

Subbing your own copy is considerably harder to do than subbing someone else's copy. You need to be self-critical and objective - neither of which are easy with words that you have crafted. It is very easy to become blind to spelling errors or poor style, especially if you are under pressure and need to submit copy quickly. It is best to leave anything you write for a few hours, preferably overnight, and do something else before trying attempting to sub your work. The interval allows you to read the copy with a fresh eye and mistakes are suddenly obvious.

How to sub
You need to be systematic when you sub and follow a prescribed checklist. This soon becomes habit and you will find yourself subbing everything your read - it can be annoying! But looking for specific errors makes an objective assessment of your own writing easier and helps overcome blind spots and bad habits. Listed below are typical problems to look out for and correct.

Typical problems

There is no need to become a pedant when it comes to grammar and spelling and start quoting from Lynne Truss's useful book, *Eats, Shoots & Leaves: The Zero Tolerance Approach to Punctuation*, but you do need to eliminate common mistakes. These make your copy appear amateurish and sloppy. What follows is not a grammar lesson, we assume you have that knowledge, but advice on common mistakes and how to get rid of them.

If, like most people including journalists, your knowledge of grammar is poor, do not be put off by the jargon, like hanging participles and such like. We have provided examples and it is usually obvious what is wrong even if you cannot give the mistake a fancy name. So let's start with hanging participles.

Hanging participles

A participle is when a verb or a noun is used as an adjective, like 'walking' and 'having walked'. A participle must have the same subject as the main verb in a sentence and when it does not, it is described as hanging. Hanging participles often occur when the writer tries to say too much in a sentence, which is another good reason to keep sentences short.

Consider this example: *Having walked the marathon route twice, George was able to plan his timing easily. Backed by some outstanding planning, particularly by his club captain, George went on to take the trophy.*

It is far better to write: *George planned his timing easily by walking the marathon twice. Outstanding planning, particularly by his club captain, meant George went on to take the trophy.*

Many writers become addicted to hanging participles and start every sentence with one. You end up with copy like this: Having joined the Conservatives in 1985, Michael went on to stand for office. Winning the county election gave Michael his first steps to political prominence. Compare the above to this version: Michael's first steps to prominence came in 1985 when he joined the Conservatives and later won a seat in the county election.

Exercise 1

Sort out these sentences:
Walking back home yesterday, a tree nearly fell on my head.
If properly secured, you should not be able to remove the cover.

Dangling modifiers

The words 'like' and 'as' also throw obstacles in the way of clarity of copy. When used for comparison, like and as should not start a sentence. As with writing good history, good journalism requires precision with words. It is much easier to say: Good journalism requires precision with words, as with writing history.

And better still is: Good journalism, like good history, requires precision with words. But not, Like good history, journalism requires precision with words.

Exercise 2

Sort out this sentence:
I strolled cheerfully along as the freight train roared past me without a care in the world.

Passive voice

Active verbs make for better copy. Consider this sentence: The ambulance crew rescued the injured climbers. It is far better than the passive form: The injured climbers were rescued by the ambulance crew. This is not to say that the passive can never be used, but your copy should contain mostly active verbs. The grammar check on most work processors can be set to highlight passive verbs which helps keep them to the minimum.

Exercise 3

Write these sentences in the active voice:
An article is being written by the journalist.
An article was being written by the journalist.
An article had been written by the journalist.
An article will have been written by the journalist.
An article would be written by the journalist.
An article would have been written by the journalist.
An article was written for me by the journalist.

Repetition and variation

Repetition of nouns in a sentence is usually the result of poor sentence structure with the writer forced to keep repeating the subject of the sentence to avoid confusion. The solution is to change the sentence structure. For example: Unless Nato forces can counter the threat from the Taliban, Nato forces will face many more years fighting in Afghanistan.

The writer cannot use 'they' in place on the second 'Nato' because of confusion with the Taliban. Instead of the repetition the sentence should read: Nato forces will face many more years fighting in Afghanistan unless they counter the threat from the Taliban.

Another device writers use to avoid repetition is to substitute alternative nouns. This is also done in the mistaken belief that it adds colour to copy. Not so, It usually confuses the reader or appears silly.

Be careful not add comment on what people say by using substitutes for say or said. There is no place in journalism for expressed, opined, declared, commented, ejaculated, exclaimed, blurted.

Exercise 4

Remove and replace the various names to make these sentences clearer and easier to read.

I will not tolerate this sort of aggression," declared the South African ambassador speaking to MPs last night. The Apartheid regime's spokesman faced a critical audience of MPs who heckled his speech describing the racist government's polices as liberal.

Martin Lewis opened the new baked bean factory in Hazelmere today. Mr Lewis, before pushing the button setting the canning plant in motion, announced that this was a turning point for Suffolk industry. Mr Lewis pronounced: "We can be sure of a long future for Acme beans today.

Pronoun confusion

Using pronouns like he, she, they, and their, avoids repetition of the noun but be careful that the pronoun is clear. For example: The Conservative Party-backed Freedom from Tax Movement will start distributing this week millions of pamphlets resembling local newspapers. They will tell voters not to support their MPs if they want tax reductions.

The second sentence with the two 'theys' is the problem with the meaning unclear. To keep the sense it should read: They will tell voters who want tax reductions not to support their MPs.

Exercise 5
Correct these sentences to remove the pronoun confusion. Note that the fault with some of these sentences is confusion between the pronoun and its antecedent so there are two possible answers

1 When the journalist saw the minister he smiled.
2 They looked at every new car dealership in town, but they could not afford to buy one.
3 The author wrote a biography of Abraham Lincoln that revealed his knowledge and sensitivity.
4 Smith was born prematurely and was so small when he was born that they thought he might not live.

Awkward construction
An indicator of clumsy sentence construction is the need to insert multiple comas to maintain sense, as in this example: Inherent in the company's strategy is the requirement, introduced before the take-over last year, to tender for increasingly larger projects, such as the Olympic construction work, that make enormous demands on planning and procurement. Confusion arises as to whether it is specifically Olympic bids or any large project that makes demands.

Consider this example: Overcoming the problems inherent in demolition of large structures with the danger of debris falling over a wide area, the company decided to adopt a step-by-step approach, using small machines, specially hired, that enable working in the constricted space on the site.

The solution is to keep it simple and split long sentences into two: Demolishing large structures poses the danger of debris falling over a wide area. The company's step-by-step approach, using hired small machines that can work in confined spaces, overcame the problem.

Exercise 6
Re-write these sentences below to make sense:

1 Tragically at the age of six, Smith's father died.
2 Extensive training on the new safety procedures was required to be attended by the maintenance staff.

That and which

The pedants will tell you the distinction between that and which: 'that' used to define and 'which' the relative pronoun. Most of us do not bother about the distinction but do avoid mixing the two in one sentence. In most cases the second that or which can de deleted. For example: In part, Manchester United's popularity can be attributed to its global marketing campaign that has boosted the value of the brand and which underlies its ability to gain global sponsorship deals. Delete 'which' to make the sentence easier to read and clearer.

Exercise 7

Every that, this, which, or it must have a clear antecedent otherwise, the meaning of the sentence can become vague.
Correct these sentence where the meaning is unclear.

1 Many people love to take holidays in Ireland. This helps the economy of the island.
2 After Joan heard the journalist speak, she decided to major in it.
3 For two months this summer, they were paving the street in front of my house.

Specialist vocabulary

When writing for specialist magazines take great care to get the terminology and vocabulary right. No matter how good your research and how accurate your story, readers of specialist magazines who are expert in their field will immediately dismiss your copy if you make basic mistakes. And when writing for a general audience why not use the right terminology too even if local newspapers do not.

Specialist terminology is not only industry specific but also country specific. A British truck driver may call his lorry a wagon. For an American truck driver, a wagon is something that goes on the railway, which he would call the railroad. In the case of road transport specialists, nothing is more annoying than using juggernaut to describe a truck or lorry – both words are acceptable these days. Juggernaut is an emotive term designed to suggest immense size. Why not be precise and say what the truck is, an 18-tonner, a 36-tonner, or a 44-tonner? Even better, say how many axles it has, a six-axle 44-tonne truck is more precise and more informative than a juggernaut. Equally, not all vans are Transit vans made by Ford; you will find nearly as many Sprinter vans made by Mercedes-Benz. Refuse collection vehicle is preferred to bin lorry. The traditional name is dustcart and still used by many in the industry.

On construction and building magazines, a dump truck is an American term for what British readers call a tipper truck. Contrary to what you read in almost every local newspaper bulldozers do not demolish houses. Bulldozers are large machines mainly used for site preparation and road building. A variety of machines are used for demolition work that are best described as demolition machines or plant unless you are writing for a specialist magazine in which case you will probably specify the particular attachments used.

Mechanical diggers on building sites, a term local journalists frequently use, were last used fifty or more years ago. The journalist means hydraulically powered, mechanised diggers best called simply diggers or excavators. And like the Ford Transit, not all diggers and excavators are made by JCB. And JCB makes of a huge range of construction equipment as well as the simple digger.

Jargon

It is very easily to shift from specialist vocabulary into jargon when writing for specialist titles. This is especially dangerous if you are unsure of what you are writing about and hope to conceal your ignorance. The hallmark of good specialist or technical writing is comprehension by any reader regardless of specialist expertise.

If you are unfortunate and have to work with government or corporate press statements, getting rid of jargon is especially important. Government-speak and corporate-speak, with obsessive use of acronyms and jargon, are not designed to inform. You need to work carefully to interpret much of the nonsense that appears in these press statements and avoid including such phrases or sentences into your copy. Here are extracts from a statement by a government minister.

The Campaign will tailor activities at a local level working through county groups that will be set up by farmers. I have made it clear there is a mandatory fallback, which could be introduced at a future date if the Campaign is judged not to be working, but we will give it our full support.

Do not take huge swathes of material like this direct from press releases and include it in your copy, even as quotes. Try to find out that they mean and state it in clear, sensible English. To use the text in an article you would need to attend to the following:
- "Campaign" carries an unnecessary capital
- the use of passive language in "will be set up"
- the redundant phrases "at a future date" and "is judged"
- adjectives like "full" that unnecessarily qualify support.

Foreign words
Do not use foreign words, like coup d'état, raisons d'être, and fin de siècle. They are pompous, outdated expressions that add nothing to your copy. Worse still, they are usually spelt incorrectly because they require accents that are hard to find on a keyboard and the formatting is lost when you send copy as text files. The exceptions are foreign words that have entered the English vocabulary, like Zeitgeist, coup, and cafe. Note the lack of accents on cafe and coup.

Editing and using quotes
Strictly speaking direct quotes should be the unedited record of what someone said taken from your notebook. In practice, using quotes is not quite that simple.

The objective of using a quote is to provide an authentic rendition of what someone said to add legitimacy and interest to your story. But many people do not talk using neat, structured, sound bites; they ramble, make false starts, or mix their tenses. Unedited, such a quote could make the speaker appear foolish and undermine the value of what they are saying. Such quotes will need some tidying. But how much? The *Times* style guide states; "direct quotes should be corrected only to remove solecisms and other errors that occur in speech but look silly in print." So, it is reasonable to sort out any obvious grammatical errors but not to render the quote into perfect English. Quoting the former president of the US, George Bush, illustrates the point. There is nothing you can do with a Bushism like: "They have miscalculated me as a leader."

Quotes not only add sparkle and life to the copy but also allow the reader to judge the value or strength of the statement. The quote must be part of the story and flow with the rest of the copy. If, as is often the case, the quotes are long, rambling, and disjointed it is best to resort to indirect reported speech quoting a phrase or two as in this sentence: Antony Jones said the British team showed "lamentable co-ordination" throughout the performance.

House style

House style is the way a publication or web site chooses to publish material designed to achieve consistency. National newspapers publish their style books which detail the rules and save journalists from reading back issues to establish whether they should use double or single quotes, and preferred spellings.

Style guides are a useful guide to do's and don'ts of good writing on the basis that what is good enough for the *Times*, *Economist* or the *Financial Times* is good enough for most local papers and magazines.

They are especially useful for guidance on correct usage and grammar. Most are available online too so you can always read the most up-to-date version. This is important, as language evolves. Within the past ten years grammar usage in print has become much more relaxed with less punctuation, very few capitals, no full stops on abbreviations, lack of accents, and now almost universal replacement of ise on words ending with ize.

Stylebooks are useful for sorting out troublesome brand names like Champagne, now usually spelt with a lower case c but still referring only to wines from Champagne. But stylebooks are not gospel. Some newspapers, such as the *Guardian*, still insist on the distinction between enquiry (an informal question) and inquiry (an official investigation) when few people know the difference and the words are now freely interchangeable. Most style guides still distinguish between disk and program in computing, and disc and programme for everything else. Few people would now make such a distinction.

Exercise 8

This exercise requires you to apply everything discussed in the chapter. Below is a press release, as issued, and typical of material you will work with. Use the information in the release to write a 100-word story for Hospital & Doctor, a web site aimed at NHS staff. For this exercise do NOT use bullet points. Provide a headline, maximum six words.

Press Release: NHS Continues To Deliver Key Priorities
The NHS met a number of key commitments on healthcare priorities at the end of last year and continues to show strong financial management, the Department of Health announced today. The Quarter 3 (October-December 2008) performance report published today shows that:

• The NHS met its target to have half of GP practices offering extended opening hours by the end of 2008. In January, over 71% of surgeries were opening at evenings and weekends, providing patients with greater flexibility and choice.

• Smokefree legislation has helped reduce rates of smoking to their lowest ever on record, with only 21% of adults smoking. We continue to see a steady decline in smoking among all groups, especially routine and manual workers.

• Progress has been made in tackling the decade long rising trend in childhood obesity. Latest data published in December showed that in 2007, there were 65,000 fewer obese children and 105,000 fewer overweight children than would be the case if the trend had continued.

• Good progress continued to be made on tackling Healthcare Associated Infections and meeting the 18 Weeks waits target.

Latest data on NHS financial performance forecasts the gross operating deficit to be £57 million at year-end, down from £125 million at the end of 07/08. The predicted surplus of £1.735 billion will stay within the NHS and will be used to improve patient care.

Commenting on the report David Flory, Department of Health's Director General of NHS Finance, Performance and Operations said; "This report confirms the excellent progress the NHS is continuing to make and its achievements in key priority areas. A strong financial position, backed by good progress on delivery, will continue to ensure high quality services for patients, particularly in the current economic climate.

"Building on our success in meeting key targets for GP access, 18 week waits and tackling Healthcare Associated Infections we are now making real progress against public health goals. This quarter, we have reduced smoking rates to their lowest on record and we are beginning to see a levelling-out in childhood obesity.

"It is not enough to just meet our key targets for healthcare, our challenge now is to raise standards even higher and deliver world class healthcare to all patients.

"During these tougher economic times the NHS, along with the rest of the public sector, will have to make its contribution to delivering greater efficiency. The NHS recently exceeded its Gershon efficiency targets and that gives us confidence that are well placed for the challenges ahead."
Ends

Revision exercise
The article below is typical of the material, usually supplied free to local newspaper and specialist magazines that the subs must deal with. It is turgid with overlong paragraphs, pompous expressions, and passive voice.

Re-write the copy below to provide a lively, well-structured item of 250 words suitable for publication. First, determine which items are essential to the story and what the lead will be, then rewrite to give the story fluency and flair. Add a headline, up to six words.

Following the complete refurbishment of the Park Fire Station Social Club funds were accumulating and being added to by members who remained generous to a fault with their donations so the committee decided it would be a good idea to purchase a holiday venue for the use of club members and their families. Station Officer Alan Clarke put the idea forward of a villa in Spain which would provide for an all year round letting period. Enquiries with our Bank were warmly received and Assistant Chief Officer Michael Beard was tasked with preparing a detailed assessment with cost analysis required by the Bank to facilitate their decision-making. They were prepared to back us financially and thought it a good idea. Over the next few months myself and Alan Clarke went on several trips to the Costa Del Sol where we looked at hundreds of properties. On our return to the UK we put a choice of several villas in various locations all within the price range that had been established on the Costa Del Sol before the committee, with literature, photographs, leaflets, and web sites and it was decided to purchase at Juan Carlos, Santana, Bergja. Consideration had to be given for the need to have somewhere that could be managed on our behalf and with that in mind we actually did not purchase a villa but a piece of land where the villa would be built. Juan Carlos, Santana is about one hours drive from Malaga Airport in a hire car, in a quaint peaceful little fishing village called BergJa. Juan Carlos is a purpose built village with laid out streets and lighting and excellent facilities. The villa itself comprises of two bedrooms with a large kitchen that is open plan on a sitting area which would have space for an extra bed if needed. There is a large veranda with a patio. We also have our own private garden to which entry is gained though a gate that has a lock. Opposite the villa and about fifty yards away is a new complex of villas which have a sport club with squash and tennis facilities, swimming pool, supermarket, and a restaurant although this has yet to be completed. The total cost of the villa which includes the fitted kitchen units and tasteful furniture chosen from a range of styles in a catalogue is £45,000. At the time of writing this has been paid for in full. We have experienced no letting problems since the villa was opened, and we charge £400 in the high season and £300 in the low season for a weeks stay in the winter months. We can also get a discount on car hire for members from Malaga airport from the agents that handle the booking and manage the villa for us. ENDS

Answers

Exercise 1

A tree nearly fell on my head when walking back home yesterday.

You should not be able to remove the cover if properly secured.

Exercise 2

I strolled cheerfully along without a care in the world as the freight train roared past me.

Exercise 3

Note passive and active work in all tenses, past present and future as these answers demonstrate.

An article is being written by the journalist

    Active: The journalist is writing an article

An article was being written by the journalist

    Active: The journalist was writing an article

An article had been written by the journalist

    Active: The journalist had written an article

An article will have been written by the journalist

    Active: The journalist will have written the article

An article would be written by the journalist

    Active: The journalist would write the article

An article would have been written by the journalist

    Active: The journalist would have written the article

An article was written for me by the journalist

    Active: The journalist wrote an article for me

Exercise 4

"I will not tolerate this sort of aggression," said the South African ambassador speaking to MPs last night. The ambassador faced a critical audience of MPs who heckled his speech describing South African government policies as liberal

"Martin Lewis opened the new baked bean factory in Hazelmere today. He said, before pushing the button setting the canning plant in motion, that this was a turning point for Suffolk industry. "We can be sure of a long future for Acme Beans today."

Exercise 5

1) The journalist smiled when he saw the minister or The minister smiled when he saw the journalist

2) They looked at every car dealership in town, but they could not afford to buy a new car.

3) The author wrote a biography of Abraham Lincoln that revealed Lincoln's knowledge and sensitivity.

4) The final sentence is a little harder. The sentence is better written: Smith, born prematurely, was so small they thought he might not live. But who does the pronoun "they" refer to? The doctors? His parents? Relatives? Friends? It is a pronoun without an antecedent.

Exercise 6

1) Tragically at the age of six, Smith's father died. This says that Smith's father died at the age of six.

The writer meant. "Tragically, when Smith was six years old, his father died." Do not make the reader work to interpret what you write.

2) The new safety procedures required maintenance staff to attend extensive training.

Exercise 7

Many people love to take holidays in Ireland. This tourism helps the economies of these states.

After Joan heard the journalist speak, she decided to major in journalism.

For two months this summer, the roads department was paving the street in front of my house.

Exercise 8

There are many answers but here is one version that emphasises the financial position simply because there is more detail easily reported than the vague generalisations about services levels. The edited story, shown on the next page, is still too weak to publish with the vague "a number of" that needs clarification.

NHS on target

The NHS met a number of its service and financial performance targets according to the Department of Health Quarter 3 performance report published today

The NHS forecasts a gross operating deficit of £57m at year-end, down from £125m at the end of 07/08. The predicted surplus of £1.735bn will stay within the NHS and used to improve patient care, the report said.

David Flory, director general, NHS Finance, Performance and Operations said: "A strong financial position, backed by good progress on delivery, will continue to ensure high quality services for patients, particularly in the current economic climate."
ENDS 98 words

Further reading

On writing and subbing
Essential Reporting: The NCTJ Guide for Trainee Journalists, Sage (2007)
Harold Evans, *Essential English for Journalists, Editors and Writers,* Pimlico (London 2002) first published 1972
Wynford Hicks and Tim Holmes, Subediting for journalists, Routledge (London 2002)
Wynford Hicks, English for Journalists, Routledge Routledge (2006)
Wynford Hicks, Sally Adams and Hariett Gilbert, Writing For Journalists by Routledge (1999)
Kim Fletcher, The Journalist's Handbook, Macmillan (2005)
McNae's Essential Law for Journalists, OUP Oxford; 19 edition (2007)
Leslie Sellers, The Simple Subs Book, Pergamon (1968)

Style Guides
Guardian: www.guardian.co.uk/styleguide
Observer: www.guardian.co.uk/styleguide
Times:
www.timesonline.co.uk/tol/tools_and_services/specials/style_guide/
Economist: www.economist.com/research/styleguide/
Daily Telegraph: www.telegraph.co.uk/topics/about-us/style-book/1435295/Telegraph-Style-Book-Introduction.html
Economist style guide print edition Style Guide, Profile Books Useful if you write for US titles. There is a section on the differences between British and American English.
New York Times Manual of Style and Usage:, Allan M. Siegal, Crown
Financial Times Style Guide, Paul Birch, Financial Times/Prentice Hall

WRITING FOR THE WEB

The web offers the potential for many more journalists to research, report, and write. The change will be uncomfortable and the web will probably have unpredicted results, but that is the nature change.

The Internet offers huge opportunities for aspiring journalists with web sites and blogs great places to get your work seen. Never before has it been so easy to promote yourself and your skill to such a wide audience. The downside is that more and more people are out there doing the same so competition is tough and rates of pay low.

To stand out your copy needs to be fresh, crisp, clean, and readable. We are back to training and basic skills and what this e-course is about. It is also why we have left the web writing chapter to last. The technology might be new and the methods of presenting copy new, but the essential skill remains the same: that of writing well.

The exercises in this, the penultimate chapter, require that you bring to bear all the knowledge and skill gained so far in the course. We have provided these exercises to enable you to practice and hone your writing skills but in this case specifically for the web. The aim is to provide short, clear, lively, and enticing copy relevant to the specified audience.

Each exercise uses a real press release, unedited and supplied here in full, as issued. The releases are not topical so for the purposes of the exercise do not contact the press agents, if they are identified, merely use the information provided. However, it may be helpful, and is certainly good practice, to check any web sites where references are provided.

These press releases contain all the usual problems: expect to find the passive voice, spelling errors, poor grammar, jargon, repetition, and excessive adjectives. Make sure you do not carry their mistakes into your copy. The same applies to the headlines: write your own headline to suit your copy, do not take the headline from the release, rarely is it suitable or short enough.

Think before you type: choose your language and vocabulary to suit the style and tone of the outlet you are writing for. Do not replicate any poor style or errors in the press releases.

Exercise 1

Use the following press release for a story on Marketing Solutions'
web site, an international site read by advertising agents, brand
managers (mainly US and Europe). Write an article for the specified
web outlet of 150 words with a headline of no more than six words.

Press Release: Co-op Travel Signs New Car Hire Agreement with Leading Comparison Site
Co-op Travel has signed a new car hire agreement with Carrentals.co.uk, which will see the cooptravel.co.uk website compare prices from over 35 car rental companies through a white label service.

The first company to incorporate the Carrentals.co.uk white label solution into their website, Co-op Travel will now offer a more integrated experience for customers, enabling them to compare a wide range of cars, companies and prices through a fully branded car hire section.

Through the new agreement Co-op Travel aims to double its car rental business in the first year.

Justin Joyce, Head of Customer Experience at Co-op Travel, says: "While we had car hire on the site before, it failed to offer the quality customer experience we need to deliver in the current market. As a result we looked to provide a more comprehensive service that would ensure visitors to our site got the best choice of prices and providers. "The Carrentals solution offered us the ability to include their full comparison service, but with our own branding throughout. The result is a far superior car hire experience for our customers, with feedback from users already very positive and bookings in the first few days of launch well ahead of target."

The announcement comes as many travellers face car hire shortages and price rises in popular destinations across the UK and Europe, as car rental companies cut stock levels for 2009 in light of the recession. The new Co-op Travel car hire service will now offer a wider choice of both large and small rental suppliers, providing more choice of cars and prices in one place.

To promote the new offering Co-op Travel has made car hire more prominent throughout its site, with customers benefiting from a fairer, broader choice of car hire options.

Gareth Robinson, managing director of Carrentals.co.uk, says: "This is the first white label agreement we have entered into, but the quality of our car hire offering is attracting growing interest from companies who want to enhance their customer experience in this area. We've invested a lot in developing the technology to deliver a first class comparison service, and we are confident that Co-op Travel will quickly see the benefits this brings in terms of sales and service." Carrentals.co.uk was voted Best Car Hire Website in the 2008 Travolution awards, and compares prices from over 35 leading rental providers including Alamo, Budget, Holiday Autos, and Thrifty.

Co-op Travel is part of the Midcounties Co-operative and is one of the largest independent travel agents, offering a wide range of holiday options.

For more information on car hire and Carrentals.co.uk visit www.Carrentals.co.uk.

What is different about the web?

Publishing, until the arrival of the web, and the plethora of companies hosting services for web users, was the preserve of a small elite taking their copy from reasonably well-trained journalists. The standards, especially in Britain, were high. The Internet means everyone can be a publisher with their own web site and blog: and it shows.

The arrival of new technology has led to the specialisation of tasks within the print industry disappearing in less than a generation. It also happened to the previous generation brought up on photogravure, lithography, and stereos, who found themselves dealing with slugs and Linotype.

Writing on the web is about multi-tasking: writing, subbing, editing, picture editing and research. It is also about writing for not just one medium, such as newspapers or magazines where the format is fixed, but a host of outlets including mobile phones and just about any other digital device. The devices that people can use to access journalistic output are unlimited.

And your readers are international, often on the move, and able to response almost instantly, to what you have written (think of Twitter). They want news, entertainment, facts, analysis, opinion - and they want it fast. This changes how you write and present your stories.

The web also means that more than words can be used: you can tell the story or add to the story with pictures, cartoons, video clips, audio, opinion polls, chat forums. Explore web sites of newspapers like the *Guardian* and other web sites for examples of the additional material possible on web sites. You will add value to your work if you supply this sort of additional material as well as copy but check that it is wanted before supplying. Be careful not to supply copyright material unless authorised.

Most people using online writers want content for websites or material for blogs. Others want someone to write an e-book or training course sold on the web. If you are a native English speaker, have access to the Internet and can use Google then you can get paid for your writing efforts selling to these web sites. Admittedly, payment may not be very much at first but if you build a portfolio with testimonials and references from happy clients then you could soon raise your rates and earn more money.

Exercise 2
Use the following press release for an article for Healthy Living Today web site.

1) Write a 200-word article with a headline of no more than six words.

2) What other devices such as video or audio clips etc, could you use on the web site?

Press release: Recession hit Britons nostalgic for a simpler time highlights Millward Brown research

As UK consumers continue to get to grips with the reality of recession, new research announced today by Millward Brown finds that they are reassessing their priorities in life and acknowledging that they don't need to spend to be happy. The research highlighted a renewed appreciation of the simple pleasures in life such as health, happiness, family and friends, home life and time.

Spending patterns are also being adjusted. The most conservative in Europe when it comes to future spending plans, more than half of UK consumers, 55 percent, are planning to decrease spending compared to a European average of 31 percent. 44 percent will maintain spend in the next year, compared to a European average of 61 percent.

Three quarters, 72 percent, feel now is the time to avoid financial risk while only 19 percent say now is the time to purchase goods, taking advantage of special offers and discounts.

Despite this, UK consumers are the most optimistic in Europe - 42 percent expect the economy to improve compared to a European average of 25 percent. This apparent contradiction suggests many people feel it will take time for economic improvements to filter down to individuals, leaving them cautious about their own spending in the short term.

The recession is also impacting the way people shop. Many people are reclassifying what constitutes a luxury, avoiding impulse purchases and screening their purchases more carefully for real value, not just for the cheapest price. They are also more reluctant to 'show off' new purchases to avoid being insensitive. At the same time it appears that people are remaining fiercely loyal to trustworthy and loved brands. Many people in the study talked passionately about particular brands that are definitely worth paying a bit more for.

While spending on big ticket items has declined, people are still spending on small and inexpensive treats to help them feel better - quality chocolate, a good book or magazine, a trip to the cinema with the family, a bottle of nice wine and a meal at home.

Perhaps due to spending more time at home, many respondents said they were spending more time using the Internet (60 percent), playing video games (22 percent) and watching TV (14 percent).

"People are looking for ways to enjoy themselves that do not involve spending money - walks in the park, going to the beach, gardening, cooking together, spending time with family and friends and talking to neighbours," said Duncan Southgate, Global Innovation Director at Millward Brown. "We are seeing a real return to traditional values and a simpler, less complicated life with purchases being screened for value and necessity."

Southgate advised marketers to reflect these new consumer purchasing considerations in their marketing activities. He concluded "brands can help consumers reduce tension by providing reassurance, being calm, positive, helpful and hopeful.

Their communications could potentially include more emphasis on some of the values people are yearning for honesty, sincerity, back-to-basics, no-nonsense and a focus on the family". The research project was conducted across 11 European countries using Millward Brown's purpose built social network research platform, IDEABLOG, to assess how consumers are coping with recession. 163 UK respondents aged between 18 and 55 (excluding people seriously affected by the recession) engaged in an online blog discussion which incorporated mini-polls, surveys and other interactive activities. A first in the research industry, this study delivers a depth and nuance unavailable in traditional opinion polling and reflects a powerful combination of quantitative and qualitative research techniques.
ENDS

Accuracy

The stereotypical portrait of the journalist pursuing a scoop, using their wits and imagination to beat rivals to be first with the story – has gained new currency with the web era. Speed and accuracy are of the essence. But the fact that you can change a story in a way not possible on a print edition does not mean you can submit inaccurate copy on the basis that someone will get it right later.

Freelances usually submit their copy to a web publisher and someone else places it on the web site. For the freelance, there is a built-in pause for checking and verifying their copy before it goes live. If you are posting copy on a live site, make sure you check everything before it goes live.

Web sites tend to put material up in all sorts of different places and while you may be able to correct that libellous mistake on one site, in the intervening period before you discovered the libel or error your story could be all over the place.

Exercise 3

Use the following press release for your local newspaper web site (specify your locality). Write an article for the specified web outlet of between 80 and 100 words with a headline of no more than six words.

Press release: Autumn Swine Flu Could Pose Havoc On Business Working Time

If a second bout of swine flu hits the UK in the autumn, the new working time rules could pose havoc on business operations, according to West Midlands business leaders.

Cathy Davies, network manager of Enterprise Europe West Midlands (EEN), part of Birmingham Chamber of Commerce and Industry (BCI), said as employees strive to cover for sick colleagues, they could well find themselves in breach of the Working Time Directive.

In liaison with international law firm, Pinsent Masons, the EEN is organising a two-hour breakfast and presentation on September 24. The free workshop will review recent developments and will explore how employers are coping.

Cathy Davies said: "The Chamber of Commerce believes that the availability of an opt out from the 48 hour maximum working week is beneficial to both employers and employees. Businesses need a flexible economic environment in order to maximise productivity and profitability. A central ingredient to this environment is a flexible labour market.

"BCI does not support a long hours working culture. However employees should have the choice whether or not to work longer hours. The freedom for employees to define their working hours, with the agreement of their employer, is of benefit to both when disasters like swine flu strike.

"Removing the opt out cannot be justified on health and safety grounds. The UK has one of the best records on health and safety in the EU and has also recently legislated to promote flexible working practices. As a result the number of hours worked in the UK is declining."

To be held at the Hotel Du Vin in the city centre, the working time directive presentations start at 8am and finish with questions and answers at 9.40am.

ENDS

Note to Editors:

Birmingham Chamber of Commerce and Industry is one of the UK's oldest and largest Chambers and represents almost 3,000 companies that employ over 150,000 people in Birmingham and Solihull. It offers extensive services to industry and commerce, having served the interests of business for over two centuries, promoting trade locally, nationally and internationally.

Exercise 4

Use the following press release for the financial advice pages of your local newspaper's web site. Write an article for the specified web outlet of between 60 and 80 words with a headline of no more than six words.

Ptress release:Fixed Rate Mortgage Margins Increase Again Mortgage lenders are showing continuing reluctance to reduce the cost of fixed rate mortgages, despite around a 30 basis point reduction in the cost of funding on the swap rates market.

The margin between the average two year fixed mortgage (5.18%) and the two year swap rate (2.04%) stands at 3.14%, the widest margin on record.

During the last month, only a couple of lenders reduced selected rates, including Cheltenham and Gloucester and Nationwide BS. However, other lenders such as Barnsley BS, Chelsea BS and The Post Office all increased rates.

Many lenders have been looking to their savings books to fund their mortgage activity, but in the same period only six accounts saw an increase in rates.

Michelle Slade, spokesperson for Moneyfacts.co.uk, commented: "Borrowers looking for a new mortgage deal are continuing to pay a heavy price for previous mistakes made by lenders.

"Margins continue to be increased as lenders look to repair dented balance sheets.

"Normal rules where lenders pass or decrease rates based on the cost of funding seem to have well and truly gone out of the window.

"Lenders have always been quicker to pass on increases rather than decreases, but many seem to be reluctant to pass on any decrease in the current climate.

"Savers had been benefiting from the demand by providers to raise money, but this demand seems to have eased.

"The average savings rate stands at 0.84% for variable rate deals and 3.42% for fixed rate deals. Lenders which fund their mortgages through this route are also taking a larger margin than ever before.

"Although tracker rates currently offer much lower rates than fixed rate mortgages, many borrowers are worried about the impact any inevitable increase in base rate will have on their ability to repay their mortgage in future.

"Fixed rates are the preferred option for many borrowers' and lenders are cashing in on those seeking a new deal.

"It appears that those looking for a new deal are subsidising the revenue lenders are losing from existing customers on low rate SVR or tracker deals, some of which are currently paying less than 1%."

Ends

Notes to Editor:
About Moneyfacts.co.uk
Moneyfacts.co.uk is the UK's leading independent provider of personal finance information. For the last 21 years, Moneyfacts' information has been the key driver behind many personal

finance decisions, from the Treasury and the Bank of England to the high street.

Our increasingly popular consumer website www.moneyfacts.co.uk helps customers make better financial decisions and gives them the ability to check the latest best buy products and to search the whole market for products that suit their individual circumstances.

Moneyfacts.co.uk also supplies best buy charts to many of the UK national and regional newspapers, with a total weekly readership in excess of 22,000,000. Moneyfacts.co.uk also provides the personal finance data that powers many UK online comparison websites. Our dedicated research experts produce three monthly publications as well as providing real time news and data services to the majority of banks and building societies. Additional information can be found at www.moneyfactsgroup.co.uk.
ENDS

Style

The web is no place for a sedate and gracious writing style. The web user visits a site, perhaps giving it only seconds of scrutiny, for information they want immediately. A feature in a print edition can rely on the reader having the time and inclination to give more time to reading and be willing to enjoy being enticed into a feature perhaps with an obscure reference in the opening line, rather like a book's opening sentence.

Writing for the web requires the story up front, fast, and clear. The web requires the essence of what news writing is about: tightly written, using straightforward language. Web writing should follow the pyramid structure of a news story with the key fact at the top and subsequent paragraphs filling out the detail. If the user is reading your copy on a mobile telephone or similar device, they are not going to get much more than a sentence or two on the screen before needing to scroll. But your story will also appear on a desk top where 300 words is visible, and then may also be archived and read later where the background and details are wanted.

There is scope for using bullet points and lists to summarise information. These devices are a quick way of listing information, are easier and faster to read, and take up less room.

Headlines should summarise the story in six or fewer words. There is no place for puns or obscure references as the headline is likely to be a key search tool for web users. The *Financial Times* is an excellent place to see good headline writing where the headline tells the story.

Brevity is everything on the web. Even a reasonable size screen allows little room for much over 150 words and web users, especially if they are browsing, tend not to scroll long pages. They might if the story grabs them but that requires good copy. More so than newspapers, web news stories are usually written in one-sentence paragraphs. The paragraph is more of a tool for text display than for grouping sentences relating to the same subject.

Exercise 5

Use the following press release for Bicycle Week's web site, the trade magazine for manufacturers and retailers of bicycles and accessories. Ignore date references for the purpose of this exercise and assume that today is today. Write an article for the specified web outlet of between 100 and 150 words and include bullet points or other devices. Provide a headline of no more than six words. Note how the release unnecessarily caps up Asda.

Press Release: Asda Launches Cheapest Bicycle In The UK
Today ASDA launches the lowest priced bike on the market as part of Pedal Power; a new ASDA initiative which aims to get more Brits on their bikes by making cycling more accessible to all.

Launched to coincide with Bike Week, (13th-21st June), these four bicycles, starting at £50* for kids and £70* for adults, are part of the iconic British Eagle label. ASDA has brought tens of thousands of the bikes so they are able to offer them at this permanently low price. Incredibly ASDA will not be making a penny from the sales such is the supermarket's commitment to getting the nation on their bikes.

Considering the average cost of petrol alone for the car commute is £454** and a London zone 1-6 travelcard comes in at

£1904 using the bike to get to and from work could save you literally thousands of pounds.

Pedal Power is all about getting people on their bikes and encouraging families to take up a new activity that they can do together. The initiative was launched by ASDA CEO Andy Bond and Olympic Champion Sir Chris Hoy - both united in their passion for cycling and committed to raising its profile as an affordable mode of transport with inherent health and environmental benefits.

Mike Logue, ASDA's Leisure Trading Director, comments, "Price should not be a barrier on whether or not to buy a bike therefore ASDA has worked incredibly hard to introduce these British Eagle bikes at market leading price on a not for profit basis. Cycling is the perfect low cost activity for all the family to stay healthy and spend quality time together."

All four bicycles are now available online and will be in store from 21th July to 9th August. For under £250 a family of four can each have a bicycle and get out on the roads.

Included in this offer are:

•26" British Eagle 18 speed Men's Mountain Bike, £70.

•26" British Eagle 18 speed Women's Mountain Bike, £70.

•2 children's 20" British Eagle bicycles, £50 each.

ASDA is also encouraging it's 165,000 colleagues to get on their bikes by signing up to the governments Cycle to Work Scheme; an initiative which rovides tax breaks to colleagues when buying a bicycle and cycling equipment under this scheme.

ENDS

Notes for Editors

•The light weight hi-tensile framed bicycles have sure grip mountain bike tyres and are perfect for everyday use. The two adult bikes also come with 18 speed gears.

•In addition to helping customers save money every day, the health and wellbeing of ASDA colleagues is a key part of the company's DNA. As well as the Cycle to Work scheme, ASDA provides its colleagues with free health and eye tests and health and nutrition advice as well as healthier options in its staff restaurants.

•ASDA is also a supporter of the Department of Health's Change4Life initiative and the lead partner for the cycling component Bike4Life.

•In the last year alone, ASDA's Sporting Chance scheme provided more that 100,000 children across the UK with free sports sessions during the school holidays, as well as vital funding for up and coming sporting talent.

• For further information on ASDA's Pedal Power initiative visit www.asda.com/pedalpower

•The British Eagle brand is already available in selected ASDA stores and has been chosen because it supplies good quality, everyday bikes.

•Bike Week runs from 13th to 21st June and the UK's largest mass participation cycling event and provides an annual opportunity to promote cycling as a source of fitness, fun and as an alternative form of transport.

Exercise 6

Use the following press release for the Retail News web site, read by managers and buyers of large and small retail stores. Write an article for the specified web outlet of between 100 and 150 words with a headline of no more than six words.

Press release: Families £12 A Week Better Off - According To Asda Income Tracker

Increase in spending power welcomed, but most people expected to save or pay off debt. The average UK family is £12 a week better off compared to June 2008 as the effect of Bank of England interest rate cuts continue to help mortgage payers. As a result the average household had £164 a week of discretionary income in June 2009, 7.8 per cent higher than a year earlier - when spending power was being hit by rapidly rising prices.

Food and drink inflation is the lowest it has been since November 2007, while inflation on utilities is the lowest since April 2008. Transport costs are down year on year but have risen in each of the last five months.

According to the latest Income Tracker report gross income rose by £10 a week in June 2009 compared with a year earlier.

After tax, average family incomes rose by £7 a week in June 2009 relative to a year earlier. However, inflation fell to its lowest level in 21 months on the consumer price index and there was a record year on year drop in prices on the retail price index.

Andy Bond, ASDA president and CEO welcomed the increase in household income but warned people may be reluctant to spend it. He said: "Despite households being £12 a week better off, and although the pace of job losses has slowed, unemployment is likely to continue rising in the coming months, affecting consumer confidence.

"Many families still face reduced household wealth and high debt levels, so although the increase in spending power is welcome, most people will probably end up saving it or using it to pay off debt. That's why it is essential that retailers like ASDA continue to fight inflation and focus on lowering prices to help stimulate consumer demand, and restore confidence as quickly as possible."

Charles Davis, an economist at Cebr who compiles the report for ASDA, said: "In June the ASDA income tracker showed the largest year on year rise since the income tracker began due to the Bank of England's interest rate cuts over the last year and the lowest rate of consumer price inflation since September 2007.

"This month's year on year comparison is exaggerated somewhat by base effects from June 2008 when prices were rocketing. But nevertheless the ASDA income tracker shows how interest rate cuts are helping households. However, labour market weakness and household balance sheet rebuilding continue to provide reasons for caution on the outlook for consumer spending."

Reduced mortgage interest payments combined with month on month reductions in the price of food, alcohol and clothing all helped to reduce the cost of items in the essential spending basket by 2.7 per cent year on year in June 2009. Overall essential spending was £5 a week lower in June 2009 compared with a year earlier. Therefore, spending power for discretionary items was £12 a week higher in June 2009 relative to June 2008.

Consumer price inflation is set to fall further towards - and quite possibly below - the 1.0 per cent mark, hence, the ASDA spending power indicator is likely to continue to rise in coming months. Although the pace of job losses has slowed, unemployment is likely to continue growing in the coming months and many households face reduced wealth levels and high debt. Therefore, increased spending power may actually end up as increased saving or debt repayment.

In the first quarter of 2009 households injected £8.1 billion into housing equity: a record net injection. This compares with an average quarterly housing equity withdrawal of £11.5 billion over the period from 2002 to 2007 (N.B. The savings ratio in 2008 was at its lowest level since 1959).
ENDS

Notes for Editors:
Family spending power is the amount remaining after the average UK household has had taxes subtracted from income and bought its basic items. It is the amount left to spend on leisure and recreation goods and services; these are listed in the appendix of the report.

A spending power indicator for the average UK household is provided on a monthly basis.

On a quarterly basis we provide the following additional spending power indicators:
Regional spending power indicators
Income band spending power indicators
Occupational spending power indicators
Household type spending power indicators

ASDA spending indicators are based on regional, income band, socioeconomic and household type desegregations using the family spending survey.

This report has been produced by the Centre for Economics and Business Research (cebr), an independent economics and business research consultancy established in 1993 providing forecasts and advice to City institutions, government departments, local authorities and numerous blue chip companies throughout Europe. The contributors to this report are Charles Davis and Douglas McWilliams.

We use official data to provide an up to date and accurate measure of spending power. From April 2009, the income tracker is based on updated official base data on family expenditure and income from the Office for National Statistics Family Spending 2008 survey; making it not directly comparable with previous versions -but up to date as possible with the latest data. ENDS

Tradition rules

The traditional rules of writing should apply online. And by traditional we means applying the rules of grammar and spelling and all the other qualities needed for sharp, accurate copy. A few minutes reading material on the web and you will quickly see that writing quality is inconsistent throughout most online news sites with passive verbs, run-on sentences, mixed metaphors, and clichés. It is not speed that causes this but inexperienced journalists who simply cannot write. Readers may not be able to identify the faults but they do notice sloppy writing that makes it harder to get the story. They will stop reading a story and they will not come back for more.

Exercise 7

Use the following press release for the East Midlands Gazette web site, a local newspaper serving a wide readership but with strong business interests, across the region. Write an article for the specified web outlet of between 100 and 150 words with a headline of no more than six words.

Press Release: £82m Contract Awarded To Clean Up One Of Europe's Most Contaminated Sites
VSD Avenue, a joint venture partnership between VolkerStevin, DEC and Sita Remediation, has been awarded the contract to remediate the former Avenue Coking Works in Chesterfield.

The £82 million contract, commissioned by client East Midlands Development Agency (emda) and funded by the Government's Homes and Communities Agency (HCA) through their National Coalfields Programme, will involve the treatment of 500,000 cubic metres of heavily contaminated soils on site.

VSD Avenue obtained planning permission for the remediation works in 2007 and has since been working on a more detailed solution to the contamination problems on site, which will use techniques that haven't been used in the UK on this scale before. This will require a uniquely designed thermal desorption treatment plant and a water treatment facility to be built on site.

The regeneration of the former industrial site is expected to start in early September and will take around five years to complete. It will involve the excavation of around two million cubic metres of material, includes the clean up of two silt lagoons, a registered asbestos waste tip and ground pollution caused by heavy metals and waste chemicals. A commitment by the project team to sustainable regeneration will ensure that most of the treated material will be reused on site.

Marcus Foweather, project director for VSD Avenue, said: "This is one of the most complex civil engineering remediation schemes in Europe and we have worked hard to ensure that the remediation works set new standards and provide a benchmark for other heavily contaminated sites. It uses some exciting remediation techniques using state of the art technology as well as focusing on sustainability and environmental issues."

Exercise 8
Use the following press release for Public Service and Local Government magazine's web site. This is a small circulation magazine read mainly by local authority officers and elected officials. Write an article for the specified web outlet of between 150 and 180 words with a headline of no more than six words. Do not forget to consider bullet points to aid clarity.

Press Release: Hays reveals recruiting private sector talent is now a priority for public sector
Hays Public Services has revealed the results of a new survey which shows that more than 80% of public sector organisations believe skills shortages in their organisation would be best filled by private sector workers.

Employers based across public services divisions including education, central and local government, housing, the NHS, charities and not for profit organisations stressed concern about the lack of commercial talent. 47% of respondents also said there are widespread skill shortages generally and this needs to be addressed in order for quality services to be delivered.

Concerns expressed by respondents identified shortages in management skills (54%) and indicated that the most valuable attributes a private sector candidate can bring to the public sector is commercial expertise (61%) and creativity (17%). Other attributes include a different drive and ethic.

The time to move to the public sector may be now, with 63% of employers confirming they have noticed an upturn in applications. Significantly 86% believe this increase is beneficial with job candidates bringing a diverse range of skills experience and willingness to adapt to new methods.

Andy Robling, Director at Hays Public Services, said: "The recession has forced people to re-evaluate their perception of a job in the public sector and they have come to realise that it offers comparable pay, generous benefits and a challenging, yet rewarding, environment. At the same time, many public sector organisations are undergoing a period of change and commercial expertise is highly valued to manage this process and drive efficiencies. Employers need to make sure they are tapping into this pool of talent. Jobseekers with a commercial background have never been more available or more willing to move."

Although almost two-fifths of public sector employers are adamant that the recession has enabled access to a pool of talent that may otherwise not have been on offer, there is also the concern that once the economy picks up many of the new workers will leave and go back to previous private sector employment, once again leaving a dearth of skills. However, of greater concern to employers is their recruitment costs, with almost a fifth claiming that this was currently their biggest staffing challenge - an increase of 8% compared to before the recession, which perhaps isn't surprising in the current climate. "All costs in an organisation are being scrutinised closely, and recruitment isn't an exception. We are looking at innovative ways to partner with our clients to deliver maximum cost efficiencies and help them to find quality candidates, at a time when they are being inundated with CVs," concluded Robling.
Ends

About Hays Public Services:
Hays Public Services is part of Hays plc and specialises in public
sector jobs including social housing jobs and a range of jobs in
education. It is market leader in the UK and Australia, and one of
the market leaders in Continental Europe. As of 30 June 2008, the
Group employed 8,294 staff operating from 380 offices in 28
countries across 17 specialisms. For the year ended 30 June 2008,
the Group had revenues of £2.5 billion, net fees of £786.8 million
and operating profit before exceptional items of £253.8 million.
The Group placed around 80,000 candidates into permanent jobs
and around 300,000 people into temporary assignments and the
temporary placement business represented 49% of net fees and
the permanent placement business represented 51% of net fees.

Speed

The number of exercises we have set you to work through in this
chapter may puzzle you, especially since they are all pretty much alike.
The reason is speed. Payment rates are low for web site work and you
must be able to write accurately, but also very fast.

Speed and accuracy come with practice. Tackle the next two
exercises, exercise 9 and 10, but time yourself. Your goal is to complete
to complete each exercise in 15 minutes: that is written, checked, and
ready to send.

Exercise 9

Use the following press release for the Daily Telegraph web site.
Write a 60-word story for the specified web outlet with a headline of
no more than four words.

Press Release: Working Up The Tiers Just Got Easier
For the first time, British Airways is offering customers flying on
discount economy tickets the opportunity to earn Executive Club
tier points to help them ascend the blue, silver and gold ranks of
the airline's loyalty scheme. The permanent change to the
Executive Club follows a successful trial after members said such
an improvement would be top of their wish list.

Ian Romanis, British Airways' head of loyalty, said: "We've been
listening to our members and rolling out a host of new benefits

for the British Airways Executive Club. This is the latest initiative and our customers tell us they're delighted we've made this change. It brings real value to members, allowing them to either move more easily up the tiers, or simply maintain their status, regardless of the type of ticket they're on."

The changes mean that Silver and Gold Executive Club members will find it simpler to maintain their status and the benefits associated with them, including access to 150 lounges worldwide, including British Airways' £60 million Galleries lounge complex at Terminal 5.

Customers in Euro Traveller (shorthaul economy) will receive five tier points whilst those in World Traveller (longhaul economy) will receive fifteen tier points with every booking. Other recent enhancements to the BA Executive Club scheme include:

• Blue members can make it to Silver, and Silvers can maintain their status by taking 50 flights.

• The ability for Gold card holders to book any route, cabin or date for double the cost of the standard redemption rate, provided they book 30 days or more in advance.
ENDS

Notes to editors:
Entry levels for tier points are:
Blue - zero points needed
Silver - 600 points or 50 flights with BA needed
Gold - 1500 points needed
The British Airways Executive Club has four million members, 1.7m of which are in the UK alone. Anyone who takes a BA flight can join the scheme and collect BA Miles, which are redeemable on flights and partner offers, as well as tier points which allow them to climb the ranks of the scheme and accrue the additional benefits associated with each level.

Exercise 10

Use the following press release for your local newspaper (specify your region) Write an article for the specified web outlet of 120 words with a headline of no more than six words.

Press release: Dairy Crest - Leading The Way With Recycled Bottles

Dairy Crest, the first dairy company to commit to reducing household packaging waste by signing the Courtauld Commitment, has now become the first in the sector to put an exciting recycling initiative into action.

In partnership with bottle manufacturer Nampak Plastics and recycler Greenstar WES, Dairy Crest has developed the UK's first milk bottle containing 10% recycled material, rHDPE (recycled High Density Polyethclyne). The bottle will be made from material collected from previously-used plastic milk bottles which will allow consumers a simple way to help the environment by putting out these bottles for recycling.

Approximately 50% of plastic milk bottles are already being collected and recycled with a significant proportion going abroad for reprocessing. This new partnership will mean that plastic milk bottles are being recycled and reprocessed here in the UK and at 10% recycled content additions, up to 13,000 tonnes of virgin HDPE plastic could be saved each year.

The familiar 1, 2, 4 and 6 pint bottles, which now contain the recycled material, have started rolling off the conveyor belts at Dairy Crest's dairy in Chadwell Heath, Dagenham, with its facility at Severnside near Stroud, Gloucestershire following suit by the end of the year. Both facilities at Chadwell Heath and Severnside supply major High Street retailers.

Dairy Crest first began working on this project using rHDPE in its liquid packaging early in 2006 with Nampak and WRAP (the government-sponsored Waste & Resources Action Programme). The original prototype bottles were launched in March 2007 and are used by Marks & Spencer in its range of organic milk.

Dairy Crest led the industry working group to develop the protocol required for commercial quantities of rHDPE material to be manufactured. Recycled content milk packaging is also an integral part of the Dairy Industry's Milk Roadmap designed to reduce the industry's carbon impacts.

The company believes the recent move to using reprocessed bottles will help raise the bar for the industry where packaging and environmental issues are concerned.

Dairy Crest Group Procurement Director, Richard Jones, says: "Delivering absolute reductions in packaging waste by next year is a key part of the Courtauld Commitment. Finding a sustainable solution has been a real challenge but we've proved that it can be done. We have worked hard with our partners to achieve this result and are proud to be taking a leading position in the industry towards minimising our impact on the environment." ENDS

Keyword Writing

The web is searchable so web sites need to include relevant material featuring keywords to get the site ranked high by the search engines. For that to happen web site owners will target specific keywords and require you to include those keywords in your article without "keyword stuffing", by making sure that it reads naturally.

Exercise 11

Write an 80 word story on bus services in your area for your local website. Include the following key words: transport, timetables, reliable service, Gateway Shopping Centre, disabled access.

Selling copy online

Most people using online writers look for content for websites or material for blogs. Others will be looking for someone to write an e-book or a training course sold online. If you are a native English speaker, have access to the Internet and can use Google then you can get paid for your writing efforts.

Admittedly, this may not be very much at first but if you build a portfolio with testimonials and references from happy clients you could soon raise your rates and earn more money. So, if you are desperate to get paid quickly for some freelance writing then it is worth checking out some of the websites listed on the next page.

You do not have to have much experience to get paid for simple articles. If you go through some of the projects posted on the sites then you will see the various rates involved. Some established, experienced freelancers charge $50/hour or more so there is money to be made although you might have to work for pennies or cents initially!

With www.elance.com and www.guru.co you have to go through a bidding process to get the work, with www.essaywriters.net you just choose from the available projects listed.

Copy outsourcing websites

• www.elance.com - the biggest and possibly the best of the outsourcing websites.
• www.guru.com - another one with plenty of writing projects listed on a daily basis
• www.essaywriters.net - they say they want graduates and you have to pass a 'test' to get onto their books
• www.peopleperhour.com - a limited number of journalists offering writing at modest rates
• www.limeexchange.com - this seems to have many low-paid projects on offer. Be warned, some projects advertised at $3 per 1,000 words.

Plagiarism and copyright

The ease with which users can copy and paste material electronically means plagiarism is rife on the Internet. Expect your copy to appear all over the place, usually without any recognition of you or the original source.

This may well happen quite legitimately too. Large publishers, including the UK's largest business-to-business publisher, Reed Business Information, insists that you sell your copyright when contributing to its titles. Reed, as owner of the material can sell or distribute the material as it chooses. Most small publishers take a less formal approach and while they do not purchase the copyright will use your material on multiple platforms, regardless. The reality is that as a freelance, you are simply too small to negotiate a decent contract so have to accept whatever terms you get.

It will not take you long to realise that most of the material on the web, like much found in newspapers and magazines, is sourced from press releases. If you spot a story you want to use, do not simply lift it from the newspaper web site, obtain the press release from its source, from whatever organisation issued the release, and use that. The press release is less likely to contain errors that other journalists or sub editors may have introduced and will probably have more detail to give your story a better angle to suit your readers.

National newspapers are not immune to lifting immense amounts of information from web sites without acknowledging their source. Just because a story appears in a national, even a prestigious newspaper, do not assume it is accurate or correct. Always check with the source and quote your source, it allows the reader opportunity to judge the value of the report.

Writing blogs

Blogs are great fun for the aspiring writer and a useful way to get your name out into the world. Unlike writing to commission, you have absolute control over the content of your blog but it is a labour of love. Potentially they are lucrative with a number of book deals evolving from blogs. But that tends to be the exception. More common are the number of people who have found themselves out of work after using their blog to criticise their employer.

Like successful journalists, successful bloggers consistently write compelling and engaging content. It takes hard work, diligence, and determination to keep that up on a daily basis but it is good practice for an aspiring journalist.

Blogs fall into three broad categories: personal where the posts read like a diary; collaborative where a number of people contribute; and topical where a theme determines the content.

The topical blog is the most popular with journalists who by training tend to report on events and people rather than themselves. And in most cases, these blogs are merely extensions of the reporter's role for their employer, such as those found on the BBC and other news service sites.

What makes a blog successful?

But the successful blogs, in terms of audience, are those that find a niche and stick with it. At the very least you will be posting weekly, and most successful sites have daily posts, so it takes considerable effort to keep the flow of material, inspiration, and ideas going. It is essential that you write about a topic on which you are passionate. Or at least a topic that fills a large part of your life, like your job.

A number of personal blogs describing day-to-day work experiences in a supermarket, or as a police officer, have ended up as books. But what impressed the publishers was the quality of writing and unique ideas expressed, not that it was a blog. It is back to good writing again and the basis of this course.

Do not be put off by talk of learning computer languages like HTML. Plenty of blog sites require nothing more than the ability to type your words into a space provided and follow the instructions to click a few buttons and post your comment. Blog design is straightforward and there is little benefit in designing your own site when there are so many useable templates available.

Unlike writing a paid commission where you are confident of a readership, with blogs there is, at least initially, no sense that anyone is reading your work. It is pretty soul destroying writing endless posts for a blog seemingly lost in the ether.

You have to work at getting your blog read. One way to make a blog popular is to make other blogs popular, so read others on similar topics and post responses: the more thoughtful the comment the better. On most blog sites, a link to your own blog will be automatically included in your comment, and the more blogs you post on, the more people are likely to visit your own blog.

Your blog's content is important when it comes to getting and keeping followers. No matter how good your blog marketing skills, dull comment will not appeal. You need sharp, incisive copy that stimulates and entertains to attract and retain readers. Blogs are not long discursive pieces, but short, pithy comments. The leader columns of tabloid newspapers are great examples of the sort of writing that works, and of course, successful blogs.

As a journalist, whatever the topic of your blog, make sure that spelling and grammar are faultless. A commissioning editor reading your bog is unlikely to be impressed with poor copy. You also need to be patient and not expect miracles. Most blog audiences are tiny but with time and imaginative copy you can expect your audience to grow.

Almost all magazine web sites include blogs by staff writers. Blogs are time consuming so there is scope to ghost write blogs for magazine staff. Your own blog, even if it has only a handful of readers, serves as good example to a prospective client of what you could do with a blog for them. And there is no harm in maintaining the discipline to write post daily or weekly while the practice will improve your writing skill.

Exercise 12
Use the following press release for the Daily Mail web site as the basis for a blog. Here is a chance to add your opinions. Write a blog of no more than 180 words with a headline of no more than six words using as much or as little of the press release as you please. Time yourself and aim to complete this exercise within 30 minutes.

Press Release: Sizzling year continues for online gift retailer GettingPersonal.co.uk
GettingPersonal.co.uk the UK's leading internet gift retailer is reporting continued growth in customer visits and sales.

Company sales to date in 2009 compared with the same period in 2008 are ahead by over 90%.

Nearly half a million customers visited gettingpersonal.co.uk in June, where were up amazing 96% on the same month last year and according to market intelligence company Hitwise, the company had nearly 30% of all the UK internet traffic generated from people searching 'fathers day gifts'.

"Outside of Christmas this June was our busiest month ever", says Co-Founder, Giles Harridge. "We shipped 46,000 items in the month."

Our customers like our impressive range of personalised and fun gifts and the fact that we deliver so quickly. Order one of our new range of personalised greeting cards by lunchtime and you'll get it the next working day. Many customers post reviews on our site to tells what they think of us - we're getting top marks - and this helps new visitors see how well our gifts are received."
ENDS
Notes to Editor:
About gettingpersonal.co.uk
•GettingPersonal.co.uk was set up in 2005 by two friends, John Smith and Giles Harridge, and quickly gained a reputation for its unusual and quirky gifts.

•At it's year end in April, the company's reported a jump in revenues to £6.3M (FY08: £3.2M, FY07: £1.8M, FY06: £0.4).
•It's now the fastest growing online gift retailer in the UK and is acknowledged by Hitwise as a top 5 in the sector Gifts & Flowers.
•The company was awarded Manchester Evening News Young Business of the Year 2008.

Revision exercises

Task 1

1) Using only the press release provided below, write an article for the International Property News web site of between 100 and 120 words and provide a headline of no more than six words.

2) Specify who you would contact for further information such as a company press agent or other company spokesperson

3) Write up to six questions that you would put to the press officer or other contact.

4) Identify another sector, web site, or publication that might be interested in this story and write in no more than 30 words: the name of the outlet, a summary of the story and why It Is relevant to that outlet.

Press release:

British home buyers who fear they may lose out due to the insolvency of one of Spain's best known developers have been given until the end of September to register their claim with the Spanish authorities, says law firm DWF.

Aifos Arquitectura y Promociones Inmobiliarias SA has gone into administration leaving 4,000 unfinished homes. Aifos was one of the first Spanish developers to open an office in the North West although the premises in John Dalton Street, Manchester closed around two years ago. The company also had offices in Trafalgar Square, London.

Aifos, which promoted itself as a 'young and dynamic' developer, was known for its ambitious schemes, luxury services and aggressive marketing campaigns. It was behind many projects in Andalucía and owned hotels such as the Guadalpín

Marbella and the Hotel Byblos in Mjias, which is now in the process of being purchased by Sir Alan Sugar.

The company reflected the glamorous side of Marbella's construction industry but it also became synonymous with the darker side too when several of its directors were implicated by an anti-corruption campaign, Operation Malaya, the results of which shocked the country.

Antonio Guillen, a Spanish lawyer with DWF in Manchester who is advising British purchasers on the insolvency of several Spanish developers, says it is estimated that Aifos has debts of over 1,000 million Euros and more than 2,000 creditors. The company filed for voluntary administration which has now been accepted, and administrators are being appointed to supervise its affairs.

He says: "Anyone who has purchased a property off-plan from Aifos or owns a property that has not been fully finished needs to inform the administrators and the court before 30 September to ensure they are included in the final list of creditors. They will need to supply any documents that can help to prove the payments made, such as purchase contracts, payment orders and bank statements.

"They should also check whether they have been supplied with a bank guarantee. A guarantee is compulsory under Spanish law, although not all developers comply, and will ensure that if the property is not finished, a guarantor, usually a bank, will refund the money they have paid plus interest. It could mean the difference between them losing all their money and getting a refund.

"Ideally purchasers should contact a lawyer versed in Spanish insolvency law who can ensure they have all the right paperwork and are properly represented in the administration procedure, as well as contemplating alternative solutions such as enforcing the bank guarantee where this has been provided."
ENDS

Task 2

You have a commission from the BBC to write a daily blog on a specified topic. Write, in 30-minutes, a 130-word post. Today's topic is: Daffodils.

Task 3

Write, in 20-minutes, a 120 word story for the website of the Halifax Evening News. You can make up details, or search the Internet for something real about Halifax. The challenge is to include the key words in a plausible article. The details for the story are below

Title: Nightlife in Halifax

Include the following key words: exciting, gay, clubbing, trains, transport, buses, safety, pubs, methadone.

Further reading

Moi Ali, *Writing for the Web, Directory of Social Change* (2009)

Stuart Allan, *Online News: Journalism and the Internet*, Open University Press (2006)

James C Foust, *Online Journalism: Principles and Practices of News for the Web,* Holcomb Hathaway Pubs (2005)

Dan Gillmor, *We the Media: Grassroots Journalism by the People, For the People,* O'Reilly Media (2006)

Mindy McAdams, *Flash Journalism: How to Create Multimedia News Packages*, Focal Press (2005)

Anna McKane, *News Writing,* Sage Publications (2006)

Frances Quinn, *Law for Journalists*, Longman (2007)

Angela Phillips, *Good Writing for Journalists*, Sage Publications (2006)

Stephen Quinn and Vincent Filak (Eds), *Convergent Journalism an Introduction: Writing and Producing Across Media*, Focal Press (2005)

Rey G Rosales, *The Elements of Online Journalism*, iUniverse.com (2006)

Richard Rudin and Trevor Ibbotson, *Introduction to Journalism: Essential techniques and background knowledge*, Focal Press (2003)

Helen Sissons, *Practical Journalism: How to Write News*, Sage Publications (2006)

James G Stovall, *Web Journalism: Practice and Promise of a New Medium,* Allyn & Bacon (2004)

Mike Ward, *Journalism Online*, Focal Press (2002)

Tom Welsh, Walter Greenwood, and David Banks (Eds), *McNae's Essential Law for Journalists*, OUP Oxford (2007)

HOW TO GET A COMMISSION

Welcome to the final chapter. This is where you face the greatest challenge. You have done the reading, practiced the exercises, and completed all the exercises: the challenge now is to launch yourself into the real world of print and web publishing and get your first commission. But you are not on your own. This chapter provides guidance on how to identify outlets for your work, how to approach editors and pitch ideas, and where you can get further advice and information to help you in your new career.

This book has concentrated on teaching you how to write effectively: the basic skill needed by all journalists. But there is more to being a journalist than writing. You need to develop your news instincts, to identify and ferret out stories. You need to be active, exploring all the possibilities that the Internet offers as outlets for your work and as a means to get work.

The market for freelance writing

Freelance journalists are the backbone of British press. A recent survey of commissioning editors found almost a third of newspaper and magazine commissioning editors said that freelancers produce half of the editorial content of publications.

The survey, conducted in mid 2009 among 200 commissioning editors by Daryl Willcox Publishing, found the influx of freelance talent on the market due to redundancies across many publishing companies mirrored increased demand for freelance journalists. Daryl Willcox, chairman of DWPub said: "Having been both a commissioning editor and a freelance journalist in the past I always knew that the freelance journalists played an important role, but this survey reveals just how much our media relies on them."

Twelve per cent of the commissioning editors questioned said freelancers were responsible for more than three quarters of their content. Almost one in five (18%) said freelance journalists supplied between half and three quarters of content. Editors cited, as the main drivers for using freelancers, the ability to tap into expert views (69%) and specific subbing skills, interviewing or production skills (62%). One in three respondents said they looked to freelance journalists to provide last minute cover.

What commissioning editors want

The freelance market may be buoyant but direct feedback from editors shows that exploiting opportunities relies on hard work, persistence, and a good work ethic. The most important requirement for editors choosing a freelance journalist is previously published work (86%) followed by recommendations (72%). Just over half of commissioning editors said titles that freelancers had worked for previously influenced their decision.

You can take some comfort from the fact that although a proven record of accomplishment is a fast track to a successful freelance career, a professional qualification in journalism does not appear to influence commissioning editors in their choice of contributors.

Respondents also cited reliability and the ability to hit deadlines as key attributes for the freelances they chose to use. As one editor wrote: "The most important thing to me in a freelance is their ability to deliver accurate, well-written copy on time. I also need them to be able to understand their brief and the readership that their article is aimed at." This may sound as if you, as the freelancer, is doing all the work. Yes, you are, but that is why you got the commission: that is what you are paid to do.

Once you are established, editors and journalists may recommend you. That is when work may begin to arrive unsolicited: but even then, do not expect a detailed brief. Commissioning editors are buying your knowledge of a sector, business, or subject. They might have a general idea of an article but they will expect you to refine the brief, identify the sources, get the quotes, and find the angle that makes the story stand out to add value to their publication or web site.

Web opportunities

The economic downturn has taken its toll in all sectors. Opportunities for journalists, even in the once burgeoning online sector, have diminished along with pay rates. It is not unusual to see advertisements offering £50 a day for online journalists, barely the minimum wage of £5.80 per hour.

New technologies have turned publishing on its head. In previous downturns, journalists have clung to their jobs, or picked up shifts the Monday following redundancy, but this time round it is much harder. Freelance shifts are drying up as papers and magazines try to keep costs down and websites re-use existing material. The old maxim that "you'll never go hungry if you can sub" has lost much of its value. New technology means reporters file to templates, add the headlines and even the images - all traditionally work done by the sub-editor.

You can no longer rely on the fact that you are a writer and never mind the technology; it is someone else's job to use the words. Liisa Rohumaa, former editor of FT.com, makes the point in an article for *Online Journalism News* when she said: "Training and relevant skills are still key, but perhaps journalists also need to think about being creative, enterprising and entrepreneurial."

"They may take on new roles as bloggers or social media experts or find themselves reorganising teams for a convergent newsroom. They may set up their own websites or come up with new ideas they trial online and then sell to mainstream media. They may have to think about being a media professional who combines journalism, PR and marketing or a sub who can design a website; or an investigative journalist, who becomes a videographer broadcasting to the world via the internet, bypassing the mainstream broadcasters," she said.

Selling copy online

In Chapter Seven, we mentioned writing articles for copy outsourcing websites. Payment is poor but it is a way to build a portfolio with testimonials and references from happy clients. And you could soon raise your rates and earn more money. So, if you are desperate for quick payment for freelance writing then it is worth visiting these websites. Some established, experienced freelancers charge $50/hour or more so there is money to be made although initially you may work for pennies or cents. With www.elance.com and www.guru.com you must bid for the work; with www.essaywriters.net just choose from projects listed.

Copy outsourcing websites:
- www.elance.com: the biggest and possibly the best of the outsourcing websites
- www.guru.com: a site with plenty of writing projects listed on a daily basis
- www.essaywriters.net: it says it wants graduates and you have to pass a 'test' to register
- www.peopleperhour.com: A limited number of journalists offering writing at modest rates
- www.limeexchange.com: mostly low-paid projects on offer with some advertised at $3 per 1,000 words. It takes 20-minutes just to type 1,000 words!

A freelance career

We are in challenging times for those trying to get a step on the ladder as a freelance or in paid employment. Even mid-career journalists face similar difficulties. Journalism is not a closed trade or profession, anyone can join, and because everyone thinks they can write and be a journalist, many do. The technology enables contributions from a much wider audience than before, and publishers and web operators encourage this new burgeoning pool of free talent. What you have to do is use your professionalism to outclass the amateurs.

The expansion of media outlets means there are now many more new and exciting ways of getting your story out. It also means there is much more to think about. Not only must you get the story, you also have to think about how best to tell it, where, and in what form. It is not just about filing 350 words any more.

But, for all the hype about technology and web based media, never forget that the story is what it is all about. That is the difference between the journalist and the amateur.

The web is also a fantastic opportunity to promote yourself. Set up a web site and include examples of your work and links to sites that publish your work. The links and examples must be up-to-date.

Getting started
In the first chapter of the book you completed several exercises that set out the basics of how to get started. We need to revisit that work you did in the exercises for the first chapter and identify your areas of interest, your expertise, and the potential markets for your work.

Choose a subject
In what subject area do you have an interest or any special knowledge? Is it poetry, sewing, railways, computers, sailing, football, photography, singing, painting, music, politics, boxing or the environment? Or another subject?

Identify an outlet
Search the Internet for web sites about your special subject area and visit a newsagent, preferably a large newsagent, and check for web sites, newspapers, or magazines likely to include a story about your special subject. If you cannot get to a newsagent check for titles on subscription web sites, like www.magazinesubscription.co.uk/ or www.subscription.co.uk/ or www.isubscribe.co.uk/.

Identify a topic
You know your subject area; you know your media outlet. Look at back issues or any archive material on the site and establish a detailed knowledge of what the media outlet uses. Work up three or four ideas that would be suitable.

Write an article
Write an article suitable for that publication so that you have material to show as a sample. No one will commission an unknown writer without some evidence of his or her capability. Aspiring writers are in a Catch 22 situation: unable to get a commission because they have no

previous published work. This means that the sample work you provide must be good and must be relevant to the media outlet: that wonderful article on embroidery is not going to impress the commissioning editor of *Rugby Today*.

Identify your contacts
Establish the names and titles of the people who commission copy in your chosen outlets. Contact these people by phone then provide your suggestions and a sample of your work by e-mail. Be brief, clear, and succinct.

You need to establish, quickly, your credentials: your knowledge of the subject, and that you can write. Each contact must be personal with the ideas and example tailored specifically to them. Never send out a general, catchall, email: it will not be read and it will not endear you to the publication.

Persevere.
Like an author of a book, expect to get loads of rejections. It is depressing and saps your confidence but journalism requires a thick skin. Most commissioning editors work by recommendation from other journalists and editors. Like any sales person, if you cold call you are unlikely to get a warm reception. Timing and luck are important factors in getting a commission. A commissioning editor stuck with a page to fill or some new web page to publish will risk an unknown writer if they have material available and are ready to go.

The business details
The last stages of the discussion for a commission should include the length of the article in words, the copy deadline, and the payment terms.

How to pitch ideas
Commissioning editors are busy and at best, your e-mail will get a quick scan prompted by your earlier telephone call. The pitch document, usually the e-mail, needs to be succinct, carrying the essence of the story in the first line. You need to know your subject and the media outlet well in order to do this.

Provide a few sentences at most with additional supporting details about who will be quoted and suggest a story length that is typical and suitable for the title. You may have to include an additional sentence to say why the topic is relevant for the outlet if this is not clear. But remember that the commissioning editor knows the market and the medium so do not state the obvious.

And finally, you need to provide your credentials and why you, and not any other freelance or staff writer should write the article. Commissioning editors are not above taking a good idea and getting someone else, whose work and skill they know, to write it. Do not specify your fee or make any demands in this e-mail: it is a sales pitch, not a contract.

Below is a typical pitch, this one sent by one of your tutors by e-mail to a magazine editor. The editor responded the following day to confirm the piece asking for 600 words at £230/1,000.

To the Editor of Builders' Merchants Weekly

Is the following feature idea of interest?

Web Sites: Selling and promotion tool or just window dressing?

My research of web sites for hardware retailers shows that most builders' merchants have a web site but many of these, apart from a handful of large-merchant sites, are little more than dated display ads and probably expensive ads at that.

The feature to include comment from merchants, such as J T Dove, that really do use their web site, as well as web providers, discussing what works on the web, how to make the web a sales tool, and the potential for online sales.

800 to 1000 words illustrated with pulls from web sites to show good and bad practice (without identifying the bad sites).

I am a freelance journalist covering retail business and attach my article "Are online shoppers price conscious?" published in Retail Hardware Monthly.

A freelance
E-mail: Agoodfreelance@the internet.com
Telephone: 01234567 / Mobile: 75643210

Getting paid

Amid all the excitement of getting a commission it is easy to forget the all important business aspects of being a freelance: invoicing and payment.

Agree the rate

Once you have agreed a commission or had work accepted, agree the payment rate. A surprising number of publications expect to make no payment for material. The National Union of Journalists publishes detailed guides to freelance rates available on its website, www.nuj.org.uk. If you are serious about being a journalist it is worth joining the union.

There is no requirement for publishers to pay these rates, and most do not, but it is worth asking for a sensible rate in the first place even if you have to accept a lower one. At least it shows that you are aware of what should be paid.

Agree a rate either for a fixed number of words, for example 600 words at £250 per 1,000 or a flat fee for material, £150 for an article or news story. The latter is preferable and avoids any argument when the publication cuts the copy and offers part payment only for what is used, not what was supplied.

Invoice with the copy

These days, most copy is filed by e-mail. Send the invoice as an attachment with your e-mail with the copy to the commissioning editor or separately to whoever handles payments. With luck, you will be paid within 30 days.

Be wary of anyone offering payment upon publication: you have done the work and if the article is accepted, then you should be paid. Acceptance of the article, not its publication, determines the publisher's obligation to pay under contract law. Monthly titles often commission three or more months ahead of publication so you could wait as much as six months to get paid. That is not unacceptable.

Your invoice should include your name, address, contact details, a reference to the article including catchline (the single word that identifies the story) and any other information such as the publication date if known.

Identify the commissioning editor, the payment rate agreed, and any other terms. Also, specify on your invoice your payment terms, which should be payment within 30 days of invoice. The invoice should be dated, either the date when submitted with the copy or the date the commissioning editor confirms acceptance of the material if this is later.

Revision exercise

It is now time for the revision exercise. Your task is to write a pitch send it to editors in a bid to win your first commission. Use the exercises in Chapter One to identify a subject, a market, and who to pitch to. Follow our advice, persevere, and success will follow. Good Luck!

Further reading

Joan Clayton, *Journalism for Beginners: How to Get into Print and Get Paid for It*, Piatkus Books (1992)

Andrew Crofts, *The Freelance Writer's Handbook: How to Make Money and Enjoy Your Life*, Piatkus Books (2007)

Katie Fforde, *Writer's Market UK 2010: Make Money Writing,* David & Charles (2009)

Anna McKane, *Journalism: A Career Handbook (Professional Media Practice)*, Methuen Drama (2004)

Barry Turner, *The Writer's Handbook 2009*, Macmillan (2008)

RESOURCES

Web sites for journalists
BBC College of Journalism: www.bbc.co.uk/journalism/
A very useful and informative site with discussion of typical issues, law and ethics

National Union of Journalists: www.nuj.org.uk/
An extremely useful site. If you work in editorial, design or photography in newspapers, magazines, books, tv, radio, public relations or new media as an employee or as a freelance the NUJ is the union for you.

Journalism.co.uk: www.journalism.co.uk/
Journalism jobs, news and links for journalists working on-line and in print media

Freelance Journalist Directory: www.journalistdirectory.com/journalist/
Load your biography and examples of your work to reach commissioning editors

DWPub JournAlert Media News : www.featuresexec.com/bulletin/
Interviews with journalists, media news, jobs, and useful stuff for journalists
Gorkana Job Alert : www.gorkanapr.com/index

Jobs for journalists including work experience and first time jobs and internships

The *Guardian* Media section: www.guardian.co.uk/media
Broad range of material on all aspects of the media

Media Accountability: www.rjionline.org/media-accountability-systems.
A Missouri School of Journalism website dedicated to world-wide media ethics

Freelance:UK: www.freelanceuk.com/
A variety of information including jobs, advice, publications, and news

Source That Job: www.sourcethatjob.com/
Job vacancies in press and public relations

Response Source: www.responsesource.com/index_journalist.php
Online resource for journalists including press releases from a wide range of companies

Source Wire: www.sourcewire.com/
Online resource for journalists providing press releases from companies

CyberJournalist: www.cyberjournalist.net/
News and other information including writing advice

Style Guides
The *Guardian, Observer, Times, Economist, Daily Telegraph (and Sunday Telegraph)* web sites all carry the newspaper style guides
Economist style guide print edition *Style Guide*, Profile Book. Useful if you write for US titles with a section on the differences between British English and American English. It also covers financial reporting jargon
The New York Times Manual of Style and Usage. useful US
Financial Times Style Guide, Paul Birch, Financial Times/Prentice Hall (2000)
Reference books

Writing skills

Essential Reporting: The NCTJ Guide for Trainee Journalists, Sage (2007)

Harold Evans, *Essential English for Journalists, Editors and Writers,* Pimlico (London 2002) first published 1972

Rudolph Flesch, *The Art of Clear Thinking* (1951)

Rudolph Flesch, *Lite English* (1983)

Wynford Hicks and Tim Holmes, *Subediting for journalists*, Routledge (London 2002)

Wynford Hicks, *English for Journalists,* Routledge; 3 edition (2006)

Wynford Hicks, Sally Adams and Harriett Gilbert, *Writing for Journalists,* Routledge (1999)

Kim Fletcher, *The Journalist's Handbook*, Macmillan (2005)

Leslie Sellers, *The Simple Subs Book,* Pergamon, (1968)

John Seely, *Oxford A-Z of Grammar and Punctuation*, Oxford University Press (Oxford 2009)

William Strunk Jr and E B White, *The Elements of Style*, Longman (New York 1999)

Grammar textbooks

John Eastwood, *Oxford Practice Grammar,* Oxford University Press (Oxford 1992)

Michael Swan and Catherine Walter, *The Good Grammar Book*, Oxford University Press (Oxford 2001)

Michael Swan and Catherine Walter, *How English Works*, Oxford University Press (Oxford 1997)

Guides to journalism

Stuart Allan (ed), *Journalism: Critical Issues*, OUP (2005)

Bob Franklin, Martin Hamer, Mark Hanna, Marie Kinsey & John E

Richardson, *Key Concepts in Journalism Studies,* Sage Publishing (2005)

Carole Fleming, Emma Hemmingway, Gillian Moore and Dave Welford, *An Introduction to Journalism,* Sage Publishing, (2006)

Roy Greenslade, *Press Gang - The True Story of How Papers Make Profits from Propaganda*, Macmillan (2003)

Tony Harcup, Journalism - *Principles and Practice,* Sage Publications (2004)

Ian Hargreaves, *Journalism - Truth or Dare?*, OUP (2003)

Bill Kovach & Tom Rosenstiel, *The Elements of Journalism - What Newspeople Should Know and the Public Should Expect*, Guardian Books (2003)

Susan Pape & Sue Featherstone, *Newspaper Journalism: A Practical Introduction*, Sage Publishing (2005)

Stephen Quinn and Vincent F Filak, *Convergent Journalism: An Introduction*, Focal Press 2005)

Janet Trewin, *Presenting on TV & Radio - An insider's guide*, Focal Press (2003)

Ted White, *Broadcast News: Writing, Reporting & Producing*, Focal Press/Elsevier, (2005)

Writing for the web

Moi Ali, *Writing for the Web*, Directory of Social Change (2009)

Stuart Allan, *Online News: Journalism and the Internet*, Open University Press (2006)

James C Foust, *Online Journalism: Principles and Practices of News for the Web,* Holcomb Hathaway Pubs (2005)

Dan Gillmor, *We the Media: Grassroots Journalism by the People, For the People,* O'Reilly Media (2006)

Mindy McAdams, *Flash Journalism: How to Create Multimedia News Packages*, Focal Press (2005)

Anna McKane, *News Writing,* Sage Publications (2006)

Angela Phillips, *Good Writing for Journalists,* Sage Publications (2006)

Frances Quinn, *Law for Journalists*, Longman (2007)

Stephen Quinn and Vincent Filak (Eds), *Convergent Journalism an Introduction: Writing and Producing Across Media*, Focal Press (2005)

Rey G Rosales, *The Elements of Online Journalism*, iUniverse.com (2006)

Richard Rudin and Trevor Ibbotson, *Introduction to Journalism: Essential techniques and background knowledge: Essential Techniques and Background Knowledge,* Focal Press (2003)

Helen Sissons, *Practical Journalism: How to Write News*, Sage Publications (2006)

James G Stovall, *Web Journalism: Practice and Promise of a New Medium*,

Allyn & Bacon (2004)

Mike Ward, *Journalism Online*, Focal Press (2002)
The practice of journalism
Julian Bowker, *Looking at Media Studies,* Hodder & Stoughton (2003)

Noam Chomsky, *Letters from Lexington: Reflections on Propaganda,* Pluto Press (2004) (updated edition)

William Deedes, *At War with Waugh: The Real Story of "Scoop",* Pan Books (2004)

William Deedes, *Words and Deedes: Selected Journalism 1931-2006,* Pan Books (2007)

Simon Jenkins, *The Market for Glory: Fleet Street Ownership in the Twentieth Century,* Faber and Faber (1986)

Phillip Knightley, *The First Casualty,* The John Hopkins University Press, (Baltimore 2004)

Phillip Knightley, *A Hack's Progress,* Vintage (1998)

John Lloyd, *What the Media Are Doing to Our Politics,* Constable (2004)

Andrew Marr, *My Trade - A Short History of British Journalism,* Pan Macmillan (London 2005)

Evelyn Waugh, *Scoop: A Novel About Journalists,* Penguin Classics (2003)

Jim Willis, *The Mind of a Journalist: How Reporters View Themselves, Their World, and Their Craft,* Sage Publications (2009)

Media law
McNae's *Essential Law for Journalists,* OUP Oxford; 19 edition (2007)

Frances Quinn, *Law for Journalists,* Longman (2007)

Media ethics
Valerie Alia, *Media Ethics and Social Change,* Edinburgh University Press (2004)
Andrew Belsey & Ruth Chadwick, *Ethical Issues in Journalism and the Media,* Routledge (1992)

Claude-Jean Bertrand, *The Arsenal of Democracy: Media Accountability Systems,* Hampton Press (2003)

David Berry (ed) *Ethics and Media Culture - Practices and Representations*, Focal Press, (2000)

Nick Davies, *Flat Earth News,* Chatto & Windus (2008)

Gustav von Dewall, *Press Ethics: Regulation and Editorial Practice,* European Institute for the Media (1997) - includes France, Germany, Italy, Sweden, United Kingdom

Tony Harcup, *The Ethical Journalist*, Sage Publications (2007)

Nicholas Harris, *The Media and the Law: a Handbook of Law and Ethics for Media Practice*, Harris Johnsson (1995)

Jeremy Iggers, *Good News, Bad News - Journalism, Ethics & the Public Interest,* Westview Press (1999)

Matthew Kieran, *Media Ethics*, Routledge (1998)

Adrian Monck & Mike Hanley, *Can You Trust the Media?* Icon Books (2008)
Kaarle Nordenstreng, *Reports on Media Ethics in Europe,* University of Tampere (1995)

Onora O'Neill, *A Question of Trust: The BBC Reith Lectures 2002*, Cambridge University Press (2002)

Denis McQuail, *Media Accountability and Freedom of Publication*, Oxford University Press (2003)

Jay Rosen, *What Are Journalists For?* New Haven, Yale UP (1999)

Robert Schmuhl (ed), *The Responsibilities of Journalism*, University of Notre Dame Press (1984)

Patterson Wilkins, *Media Ethics*, McGraw Hill (1998)

War reporting
Chris Cramer, *Dying to Tell the Story - The Iraq War and the Media: A Tribute*, International News Safety Institute (2003)

David Domke, *God Willing? Political Fundamentalism in the White House, the 'War on Terror' and the Echoing Press*, Pluto Press (2004)

Howard Friel & Richard Falk, *The Record of the Paper: How the New York Times misreports US foreign policy*, Verso (2004)

Phillip Knightley, *The First Casualty - From the Crimea to the Falklands: The War Correspondent as Hero, Propagandist and Myth Maker*, Pan Books, (1989)

Jake Lynch, *Reporting the World - A Practical Checklist for the Ethical Reporting of Conflicts in the 21st Century*, Conflict & Peace Forums (2002)

David Miller (ed) *Tell Me Lies - Propaganda and Media Distortion in the Attack on Iraq*, Pluto Press (2004)

Greg Philo & Mike Berry, *Bad News From Israel,* Pluto Press (2004)

Sheldon Rampton and John Stauber, *Weapons of Mass Deception - The Uses of Propaganda in Bush's War on Iraq*, Robinson (2003)

Children and the media
Norma Pecora, Enyonam Osei-Hwere & Ulla Carlsson, *African Media, African Children*, Unesco Clearinghouse Yearbook (2008)

Jenny Kitzinger, *Framing Abuse: Media Influence and Public Understanding of Sexual Violence Against Children*, Pluto Press (2004)

Cecilia von Feilitzen & Ulla Carlsson, *Promote or Protect? Perspectives on media Literacy and Media Regulations*, Unesco Clearinghouse Yearbook (2003)

Sarah McCrum & Lotte Hughes, *Interviewing Children: A guide for journalists and others*, Save the Children (2003)

Peter McIntyre, Putting *Children in the Right: Guidelines for journalists & media professionals, International Federation of Journalists* (2002)

Sonia Livingstone & Moira Bovill, *Children and their Changing Media Environment: a European Comparative Study*, Lawrence Erlbaum Associates (2001)

Anura Goonasekera, *Children in the News: Reporting of Children's Issues in Television & the Press in Asia*, Asian Media, Information and Communication Centre (2001)

Mike Jempson & Charlotte Barry, *Children, Violence & the Media in an Expanding Europe*, PressWise/IFJ (2001)

ABOUT THE AUTHORS

Sally Nash

As a teenager I loved reading magazines (anything from Bunty to Jackie) and was interested in fashion. Initially I was attracted to the idea of doing a course on fashion journalism but eventually decided to study for a degree in French literature first. My interest in journalism while growing up was reinforced by the knowledge that my father, who was in the retail trade, had always wanted to be a news reporter, but had not had the opportunity to pursue this love. My interest in journalism waned a little at university and I eventually opted for a PGCE as a route to the more secure career option of teaching. I ended up teaching primary school children in Brent, which I did for two years, but knew in my heart of heart that this wasn't the career for me long-term. A friend from university had finished a 17-week intensive course at Reed Business Publishing (as it was named then) on periodical (magazine) journalism and suggested that I did it too. I felt immediately at home writing news, interviewing and experimenting with my writing style on features. After teaching, journalism seemed the ultimate in freedom – I was allowed to go out of the office without a bell ringing (teachers are ruled by bells!) and nobody questioned where I was or what time I would be back. As long as I got the story. I have concentrated on news writing for a wide variety of publications and even though I am now freelancing, news takes up most of my time. Nothing beats the feeling of digging for a controversial story, and eventually seeing it in print.

Dean Stiles

I read William L Shirer's book, *The Rise and Fall of the Third Reich*, when I was 14 and was so inspired I never wanted to be anything but a journalist. Impatient to start a career when at university I auditioned successfully as a radio journalist but was told to come back when I had finished my degree. That finished, instead of a radio career, I found a job as a trainee technical writer – inexplicably on a huge salary. The training proved invaluable, but bored with technical writing I sat the entrance test to join a leading South African daily newspaper as a trainee. I impressed the newspaper editor with my 100% score in the hour-long general knowledge test, but one look at my salary, three times the pittance paid to trainee journalists, and the newspaper turned me down. Undaunted, and with the optimism and confidence of youth, I emigrated to Britain and was soon writing for a DIY magazine, then a building magazine, and in the 80s joined Britain's largest business publisher where I spent 14 years on weekly newspapers and web sites for the road transport industry. A move to a farm in the west of Ireland set me on the freelance road again – I had already spent a year as a freelance a few years before – which has kept me busy since, writing about environmental matters, waste, construction, building, transport, vehicles, and energy. But the love of history, which is why I read Shirer's book in the first place, has stayed with me and I combined that with my love of journalism by working on a masters dissertation about British newspaper coverage of the Irish War of Independence.

INDEX

Printed in Great Britain
by Amazon.co.uk, Ltd.,
Marston Gate.